Joseph Swain

Experimental Essays on Divine Subjects, in Verse and Prose

And hymns for Social Worship

Joseph Swain

Experimental Essays on Divine Subjects, in Verse and Prose
And hymns for Social Worship

ISBN/EAN: 9783744780551

Printed in Europe, USA, Canada, Australia, Japan

Cover: Foto ©Thomas Meinert / pixelio.de

More available books at **www.hansebooks.com**

EXPERIMENTAL ESSAYS

ON

DIVINE SUBJECTS,

IN

VERSE AND PROSE:

AND

HYMNS

FOR

SOCIAL WORSHIP.

By JOSEPH SWAIN,
AUTHOR OF REDEMPTION, A POEM.

Sing Praises unto our God, for it is pleasant; and Praise is comely. Let the Children of Zion be joyful in their King.

They shall abundantly utter the Memory of thy great Goodness, and shall sing of thy Righteousness.

All thy Works shall praise thee, O Jehovah, and thy Saints shall bless thee.
PSALMS.

LONDON.
PRINTED FOR THE AUTHOR:
SOLD BY J. MATHEWS, N° 18, STRAND.
MDCCXCI.

PREFACE.

MUSIC is harmony of found; Poetry is mental mufic, or the expreffion of ideas in an harmonious, beautiful, and ftriking manner: but thofe ideas muft be firft conceived in the mind by a natural gift, which none but God can beftow, or they can never be fo expreffed as to delight the ear and heart at once. Strength and clearnefs of thought, with aptnefs of expreffion, muft all unite in order to produce true Poetry.

Almoft any man of common fenfe may acquire, by application of mind, fome tafte for Poetry, as far as reading it with pleafure, and forming a tolerable judgment of its qualities, extend: but a poet, made by rules which men have laid down, who, though they might be genuine poets, never made themfelves fo, is as likely to be ufeful and happy in the exercife of his talents, as an artift who fhould choofe to employ

ploy himself in painting dainty and curious dishes for the entertainment of a number of hungry men returning from labour. Almost all the prophets in the Old Testament were poets; and in the poetical style a great part of the Scriptures were originally written, as we are informed by our most learned Hebræans, particularly Dr. Lowth, the late bishop of London, who has given us an excellent translation of Isaiah's prophecies in irregular blank verse. But, even without the assistance of a metrical translation, our English Bible abounds with instances of the most striking and beautiful poetry. The Song of Moses is a master-piece of sublimity in this way; and there are thoughts in the Song of Deborah, Hannah, David's Elegy over Saul and Jonathan, the Psalms, and all the Prophecies, as far exceeding the best of our modern poets as the flight of an eagle exceeds the fluttering of a sparrow. If poetry had not been a proper channel for the conveyance of divine truth into the heart of man, the divine Former of the heart of man, and Author of language, would not have made choice of it for that purpose, as he certainly has done. Harmony is one of the laws of universal nature; the answering of all stringed instruments of music to the key-notes of each other is a striking instance of this truth; and the confusion which reigns in the minds of most men, and too frequently rages in the minds of all, is as actually the fruit of sin as sickness,

sickness, sorrow, or even death itself; for it is certain, were the mind perfectly holy, it would always think with perfect harmony and order. These observations may perhaps be sufficient to remove the unjust idea which some serious, and otherwise sensible persons have imbibed respecting poetry, who suppose it is not solemn enough for the most spiritual and sacred subjects.

As for the observations of learned and great men, who have, with all their learning and greatness, been strangers to real experimental religion, and who have therefore asserted that divine and spiritual truth is not a subject fruitful enough to employ the talents of a genuine poet, their ignorance is so prominent on the face of their assertions, that it is always the first feature in their character which presents itself to an eye enlightened by the Spirit of truth. The holy scriptures are an everlasting and irrefragable refutation of all such worldly wise men's opinions on the subject.

The following short Essays in verse and prose, composed on different branches of divine truth, it is hoped may suit the circumstances of plain Christians, who, though they have few opportunities of reading long treatises, can spare five minutes now and then

to

to catch a thought on what they love beſt, and go on their way rejoicing.

The Hymns for ſocial worſhip were written for a weekly meeting of that kind; and were, for the moſt part, occaſioned by the friendly meeting for the uſe of which they were deſigned.

CONTENTS.

	Page
CONVERSION and Death of Poor Joseph	1
Comfort under Affliction	6
Description of Christ	8
Seeking an absent God	11
A Hymn	13
Sudden Thought in a sweet Frame of Mind	15
On Time and Eternity—For New-Year's Day	17
The Flower	20
On Psalm xxiv.	22
Christ the Way to God	24
On Faith	26
On Hope	31
The Wells of Salvation	36
What must we do to be joyful?	38
Praise for Salvation	40
Praise for a complete Saviour	41
A Prospect of the Last Day	42
Admiration and joyful Expectation	43
The Coming of Christ to Judgment	44
Communion with Saints above	45

CONTENTS.

A Prospect of the Resurrection	47
Christian Encouragement	48
Praise for Redeeming Love	49
A Responsive Hymn	51
The Grace of Christian Love	52
Christ the only Refuge for lost Sinners	53
A Soul melted with Redeeming Love	54
Second Part	55
The Christian's Company and Employment	55
The Conversion of a Sinner	57
An encouraging Prospect for Believers	58
The Soul resisting Temptations	59
Holy Confidence	60
The Coming of Christ anticipated	61
New Covenant Joy	62
The Courage of Faith	66
The Gift of divine Peace	67
Heaven will make Amends for all	ibid.
The Fruits of pardoning Grace	68
The dying Love of Christ	69
The Assurance of Faith	71
The Pilgrims' Song	72
Mutual Encouragement	73
The Way, Hope, and End, of a Christian	74
After Prayer	75
The Triumph of Faith	77
Christian Travellers	78
Faith feeding on redeeming Love	79

Admiration

Admiration and **Confidence**	80
Adoration of the **Redeemer**	81
Praise to the King of **Zion**	82
The Privileges of a Citizen of Zion	83
Christ's unparalleled Love	85
The same	87
The Garden of Grace	90
Help against the Fear of Death	91
The Harmony of Creation and Redemption	92
Christians have Reason to sing	95
A Christian Welcome	96
On the Birth of Emmanuel	97
Christians, look homeward	98
A Day of Christian Hope	99
A Day of Christian **Conflict**	100
An Answer to one inquiring—What is harmless?	102
Elegiac Thoughts on the Death of Mr. and Miss Dawson	103
A Sinner's Conversion	105

PRACTICAL AND EXPERIMENTAL ESSAYS,

ON DIFFERENT SUBJECTS, IN PROSE.

On Divine **Truth**	107
On Divine **Zeal**	119
On Christian Watchfulness	121

On Communion with God - - 126
A Remark or two on the Scripture Doctrine of
    Election - - - - - 128
On the Evidence of Divine Grace - 130
A few Thoughts on social Religion - 133
Sentences and Observations on Christian Ex-
    perience and Practice - - - 142
On Wisdom - - - - - 165
On common Life - - - - 167

EXPERIMENTAL

EXPERIMENTAL ESSAYS.

CONVERSION AND DEATH
OF
POOR JOSEPH.

WAS it a chance; or the unerring hand,
Which (holding all things at supreme command)
Gives the bright sun to cheer a world with light,
And clothes in black'ning shades the dreary night;
That bid th' event recorded here revolve?
Christian—thy heart can soon this query solve!

A poor man cloth'd in rags, and short of wit,
Was one day strolling careless through the street:
A knot of yarn across his shoulders hung,
And trail'd behind him as he walk'd along;
Little he thought that he possess'd a soul,
Or whose the power that bids the seasons roll:
When sent on simple errands he could go;
Nought else he knew, or aught desir'd to know:

Alike

Alike of things in heav'n, or things on earth,
Of what begets events, or gives them birth,
Listless, he trudg'd along till, with the sound
Of music rous'd, he starts, and gazes round—
Where he perceives a full assembled place,
And enters, gaping with unmeaning face.
(O Lord of hosts, how wond'rous are thy ways!—
Sucklings and babes shall celebrate thy praise,
While men of honour and of wisdom lie
Bury'd by sin in endless misery!
Well did the great apostle truly say,
Not many rich or mighty love the way;
The wisdom of the Lord is foolishness
To those who proudly scorn the way of peace:
So is their wisdom to the soul that knows
That peace which from a wounded Saviour flows.)
Above the rest, a servant of the Lord
Stood to proclaim the everlasting word;
Who, with a pause, open'd the sacred book;
Then, with a voice profound and speaking look,
Pronounc'd that faithful word—that Christ came down
From heav'n's bright mansions and his Father's throne,
And put on mortal flesh, that he might save
A sinking world from an eternal grave;
Yea, how he for the chief of sinners dy'd,
And ev'ry claim of justice satisfy'd *.

* 1 Tim. i. 15.

Poor Joseph trembled, while he heard him speak
Of wrath to come, as if his heart would break:
Till through his soul he felt the silver sound
Of sweet salvation and a ransom found.
Struck with astonishment, he fix'd his eyes
Full on the preacher; and with glad surprize
Drank down the joyful news with greedy ears,
Which reach'd his heart, and fill'd his eyes with tears.
The service ended, Joseph trudg'd away,
And thus within himself was heard to say:
" Joseph was never told of this before!
Did Jesus Christ, the mighty God, whose pow'r
Made heav'n and earth and all things, come and die
To save poor helpless sinners, such as I?
Why this is brave! And, if all this be true,
Who knows but Jesus dy'd for Joseph too?"
Soon after this a message from on high
Was sent to warn poor Joseph he must die:
A burning fever rag'd thro' all his veins,
And rack'd his body with a thousand pains.
Ye who delight the paths of sin to tread
Attend poor Joseph to his dying bed,
And listen to the language of his heart,
When soul and body were about to part.
No rich variety of speech he knew,
Heart-sprung and simple were his words, tho' few:
Jesus, and Jesu's love, was all his theme—
Sufficient proof that Jesus had lov'd him!

B 2   And,

And, while with pain from side to side he roll'd,
He these great things in little accents told:
" Joseph's so vile, there cannot be a worse,—
Joseph deserves God's everlasting curse;
The chief of sinners Joseph is indeed;
But did not Jesus for such sinners bleed?
I heard one say that Jesus was a friend
To poor lost sinners, whom he would defend
From God's just vengeance and the pit of hell:
And, if a friend of sinners, who can tell
But Joseph may be one whom Jesus loves?"
But, while poor Joseph thus his interest proves,
One standing by, with cautious tone, replies:
" But, Joseph, we are told by one that's wise,
That nothing's so deceitful as the heart,—
How do you find yourself about that part?
Remember what the word is to all men,
None can be sav'd but who are born again:
Have you no token thereabout for good?
No relish, no desire, for heavenly food?
Have you no inward evidence, to prove
That you are lov'd with everlasting love?
'Tis a great thing to be an heir of heav'n,—
To see your sins, and see them all forgiv'n;
To have your soul redeem'd with precious blood,
And as a pilgrim walk the heav'nly road;
To tread the path of holiness below,
And drink the streams from Zion's rock that flow;

To live by faith upon the Son of God,
To own his sceptre and to kiss his rod;
To die to sin and live to righteousness;
To be possess'd of covenanted peace;
To trust for life in Christ, and Christ alone:
And none but such shall sing around his throne."
Poor Joseph listen'd, and with artless tongue
Resum'd the burden of his former song:
" Joseph has nothing for himself to say,—
He's deep in debt, and nothing has to pay:
Joseph's a sinner,—Jesus came from heav'n,
And shed his blood, that sins might be forgiv'n:
Jesus did die to set poor sinners free—
And who can tell but Jesus dy'd for me?
Joseph desires to love him for this love,—
And why not Joseph sing his praise above?"
Thus he went on, till, almost sunk beneath
His burning pains, he stopp'd to gasp for breath.
Now each one thought—'Tis done; poor Joseph dies!
Groaning he clos'd, or seem'd to close his eyes.
His pulses languid, and his struggles few,
Eternity was all he had in view.
Mean while, in came that servant of the Lord
Who first in Joseph's ears proclaim'd the word;
Ghastly and pale, between the jaws of death,
Just ready to resign his feeble breath,
Upwards he look'd—and, trembling with surprise,
The briny moisture starting in his eyes,

" Sir,

"Sir, is it you?" with quiv'ring lips, he cry'd;
" 'Twas you that told me first how Jesus dy'd
For sinners such as Joseph, weak and poor,
That seek the bread of life at mercy's door;
Oh pray for Joseph to that loving Lord!
Tell him that Joseph trusts his faithful word;
And loves him as the sinner's only friend,
Who dy'd his chosen people to defend."
He pray'd: poor Joseph held his hand the while,
Press'd it, and thank'd him with a peaceful smile;
Then from his pillow took a purse of gold:
" This was (said he) to keep me when grown old;
Which for the poor belov'd of Jesus take,
And tell 'em Joseph lov'd them for his sake."
Then calmly met th' uplifted hand of death,
Bless'd the kind Saviour with his fleeting breath,
And dy'd!—With tears the preacher left the place,
And Joseph's gone to sing redeeming grace!

COMFORT UNDER AFFLICTION.

HOW light (while supported by grace)
   Are all the afflictions I see,
To those the dear Lord of my peace,
   My Jesus, has suffer'd for me!
To him ev'ry comfort I owe,
   Above what the fiends have in hell;
And shall I not sing as I go,
   That Jesus does ev'ry thing well?

That

That Jesus, who stoop'd from his throne
   To pluck such a brand from the fire;
A wretch that had nought of his own,
   Not even a holy desire!
My only inheritance sin,
   A slave to rebellion and lust;
Polluted without and within,
   A child of corruption and dust.

Such was I when Jesus look'd down,
   When none but himself could relieve:
What could I expect but a frown?
   But he graciously smil'd, and said, "Live!"
And shall I impatiently fret
   And murmur beneath his kind rod?
His love and his favour forget,
   And fly in the face of my God?

Oh no; in the strength he has giv'n,
   And pledg'd his own word to bestow,
I'll fight thro' my passage to heav'n,
   And sing of his love as I go!
He'll purge away nought but my dross:
   Then let him afflict; I'll adore,
And cheerfully bear up, the cross
   My Master has carry'd before!

A DESCRIPTION OF CHRIST,

BY HIS GRACES AND POWER.

FROM SOLOMON'S SONG.

O Thou in whose presence my soul takes delight,
   On whom in affliction I call;
My Comfort by day, and my Song in the night,
   My Hope, my Salvation, my All!
Where dost thou at noon-tide resort with thy sheep,
   To feed on the pasture of love?
For why in the valley of death should I weep,
   Or alone through the wilderness rove?

O why should I wander an alien from thee,
   And cry in the desert for bread?
Thy foes will rejoice when my sorrows they see,
   And smile at the tears I have shed.
Ye daughters of Zion, declare, have ye seen
   The Star that on Israel shone?
Say if in your tents my Beloved has been,
   And where with his flocks he is gone?

This is my Beloved, his form is divine,
   His vestments shed odours around;
The locks of his head are as grapes on the vine,
   When autumn with plenty is crown'd.

The roses of Sharon, the lilies that grow
    In the vales on the banks of the streams,
On his cheeks in the beauty of excellence blow;
    His eyes are as quivers of beams!
His voice, as the sound of the dulcimer sweet,
    Is heard through the shadows of death;
The cedars on Lebanon bow at his feet;
    The air is perfum'd with his breath.
His lips as a fountain of righteousness flow,
    That waters the garden of grace;
From which their salvation the Gentiles shall know,
    And bask in the smiles of his face.

Love sits in his eyelids, and scatters delight
    Through all the bright mansions on high;
Their faces the cherubims veil in his sight,
    And tremble with fulness of joy.
He looks, and ten thousands of angels rejoice,
    While miriads wait for his word;
He speaks—and eternity, fill'd with his voice,
    Re-echo's the praise of her Lord.

His Vestment of righteousness who shall describe!
    Its purity words would defile:
The heav'ns from his presence fresh beauties imbibe,
    And earth is made rich by his smile.
Such is my Beloved.—In excellence bright,
    When pleas'd, he looks down from above,
Like the morn, when he breaks from the chambers of light,
    And comforts his people with love.

But when, arm'd with vengeance, in terror he comes,
  The nations rebellious to tame ;
The reigns of omnipotent pow'r he assumes,
  And rides in a chariot of flame.
A two-edged sword from his mouth issues forth,
  Bright quivers of fire are his eyes ;
He speaks—the black tempests are seen in the north,
  And storms from their caverns arise.

Ten thousand destructions, that wait for his word,
  And ride on the wings of his breath,
Fly swift as the winds at the nod of their Lord,
  And deal out his arrows of death.
His cloud-bursting thunders their voices resound
  Through all the vast regions on high ;
Till from the deep center loud echo's rebound,
  And meet the quick flames in the sky.

The portals of heav'n at his bidding obey,
  And expand ere his banners appear ;
Earth trembles beneath, till her mountains give way ;
  And hell shakes her fetters with fear.
When he treads on the clouds as the dust of his feet,
  And grasps the big storms in his hand,
What eye the fierce glance of his anger shall meet,
  Or who in his presence shall stand !

SEEKING

SEEKING AN ABSENT GOD.

WHERE shall a roving creature find
A center for a restless mind?
Shall nature open all her stores;
With all the treasures of the seas and shores
    My heart, my wishes bind?
    The rolling seas, the bending skies,
The lively birds that warble thro' the air
    Convey no pleasure to my eyes,
Into my ears no heav'nly music bear:
    In these I seek, but cannot find,
    A balm to heal a wounded mind.

The smiling hills, the fruitful vales,
The flow'ry garden, whence exales
    A thousand sweet perfumes,
In vain their varied stores unfold;
My eyes in these no charms behold:
    The rose unnotic'd blooms:
In these I seek, but cannot find,
A balsam for a wounded mind.

To social converse next my thoughts I bend,
    And seek for consolation there;
But in the face of ev'ry faithful friend
    Read, " Comfort dwells not here:"
Then to the living works of those long dead
I fly, and these amuse my head;

But still, alas! my heart is cold:
My eager eyes I roll from page to page;
The shining poet, and the learned sage;
   But strangely all their aid withhold;
In these I seek, but cannot **find**,
A balsam for a wounded mind.

At length I trace the heav'nly road,
And turn my thoughts from earth to God;
And, to extract the galling sting of care,
Attempt the pow'r of fervent pray'r.
Here, to a dying Saviour's flowing veins
   (Drawn by the Spirit's heav'nly art)
I fly, and in contrition's humble strains
   Pour out the sorrows of my heart.

'Tis here my weary soul is blest
With sweet uninterrupted rest:
'Tis here I lay my burthen down;
Here, thro' the cross, behold the crown;
And from Emmanuel's sorrow's see
Eternal pleasures spring for me.

'Tis from His bleeding wounds and dying groans I feel
That love dissolves a heart of steel;
And all the sweets of peace and pardon prove
From the bright wonders of redeeming love;
   'Tis here I seek, and here alone I **find**,
   A healing balsam for a wounded mind.

                             Here

Here I can look, and look again,
Till, swimming in a sea of bliss, I lose the sense of pain;
Here, with enlighten'd eyes, for ever gaze,
'Till wonder's lost in brighter wonder's blaze:
'Tis in this book of life and love
In crimson lines I read my name;
And what they feel, and what they sing above,
I know I soon shall feel—I soon shall sing the same.

Now in the rolling seas and bending skies
A thousand unseen beauties rise,
And speak their great Creator's pow'r:
The lively birds, that warble thro' the air,
In all their varied notes declare
His goodness every hour;
Nature, in all her forms, his love displays,
And with ten thousand different tongues proclaims his boundless praise.

A HYMN.

ON the wings of faith uprising,
  Jesus crucify'd I see;
While his love, my soul surprising,
  Cries, I suffer'd all for thee!

Then, beneath the cross adoring,
  Sin does like itself appear;
When, the wounds of Christ exploring,
  I can read my pardon there.

Here I'd feast my eyes for ever :
  While this balm of life I prove,
Every wound appears a river
  Flowing with eternal love!

As the sea, in restitution,
  Renders filthy waters clear;
Wash'd in this from deep pollution,
  Sinners white as angels are.

Here, the shades of guilt controlling,
  Morning dawns from blackest night;
Jesu's eyes, in darkness rolling,
  Beam with everlasting light!

Sorrow proves the spring of pleasure,
  War becomes the seed of peace,
Poverty the source of treasure,
  Anguish teams with boundless bliss!

Angels here may gaze and wonder
  What the God of love could mean
When he tore the heart asunder
  Never once defil'd with sin!

Who can think without admiring?
  Who can hear and nothing feel?
See the Lord of life expiring,
  Yet retain a heart of steel?

A SUDDEN THOUGHT

IN A SWEET FRAME OF MIND.

MY soul, whene'er thou shalt arrive
On those bright hills where angels live,
What object first will draw thine eyes?
And where wilt thou begin thy joys?

Methinks when I (released from sin)
My everlasting work begin,
When on my new-fledg'd wings I rise,
And tread the shores beyond the skies;

I'll run through every golden street,
And ask each happy soul I meet
" Where is the Lord whose praise you sing?—
Direct a stranger to the King."

I'll search the blissful mansions round,
Nor rest till I my Lord have found,
Till on his wounded side I gaze,
And see my Saviour face to face.

There will I fix my wond'ring eyes;
There I'll begin eternal joys;
And look and love away my soul,
While everlasting ages roll!

BLESSED ARE THE DEAD THAT DIE IN THE LORD.—
Rev. xiv. 13.

WHAT is it for a saint to die,
   That we the thought should fear?
'Tis but to pass the heav'nly sky,
   And leave pollution here.

True, Jordan's stream is wond'rous deep,
   And Canaan's walls are high;
But he, that guards us while we sleep,
   Can guide us when we die.

A parting world, a gaping tomb,
   Corruption and disease,
Are thorny paths to heav'n our home,
   And doors to endless bliss!

Eternal glory just before,
   And Jesus waiting there,
A heav'nly gale to waft us o'er—
   What have the saints to fear?

Why should we shrink at Jordan's flood,
   Or dread the unknown way?
See, yonder rolls a stream of blood
   That bears the curse away!

Death lost his sting when Jesus bled;
   When Jesus left the ground,
Disarm'd, the king of terrors fled,
   And felt a mortal wound!

And

And now his office is to wait
    Between the saints and sin,
A porter, near the heav'nly gate,
    To let the pilgrims in.

And, though his pale and ghastly face
    May seem to frown the while,
We soon shall see the King of grace,
    And he'll for ever smile!

ON TIME AND ETERNITY.

FOR NEW-YEAR'S-DAY.

HARK! in the ear of reason, what deep sound
So solemnly to recollection calls?
It is the voice of time, whose rushing wings
Call to attention, as he passes by,
And wake the sluggard, as he lies supine
On his soft pillow: Nor do ev'n the wise
And diligent escape reproof from him,
Who never varies in his steady course.

  Is Time gone by? yes, twelve succeeding months,
Improv'd or unimprov'd, are all revolv'd
Since the last year clos'd its account in shades.

  Fellow immortals, up! and overtake
The universal warner, lest he turn—
Whet his broad scythe; and, by divine command,
                                   Mow

Mow down your hopes, unripe; and, unprepar'd,
Summon you sudden to the awful bar
Where *Justice* sits, who will not take a bribe;
But, with impartial hand and heart unmov'd,
To holy saints or harden'd infidels
Deals life eternal, or eternal death!
We live but moments; and a moment soon
Will cut the strings that by appointment hold
Th' imprison'd soul in its corporeal cage.
Then should experience be a living clock,
And ev'ry breath a moving dial's hand,
To point us to the hour when we must die;
While every blessing we through time receive
Should, as a nimble finger, lead the mind
Up to its author God—of good the source.

But *whence is Time?* and what his errand here,
That his incessant voice attention claims?

From God he comes, the sov'reign Lord of all,
To measure man's existence here on earth,
And waft him from the cradle to the grave.
Swift, on his wings, he bears us through the maze
Of life's short race, its pleasures and its pains;
Till our appointed moment to depart;
Then drops us deep into eternity:
And what's eternity? 'tis all the past
And all the future, seeming to unite
And render now a point unseen by man.

And

And yet this *now*'s the hour in which we dress,
That we may stand before the awful Judge
Of quick and dead, in robes of heav'nly dye;
Fit to attend the marriage of the *Lamb*;
Or, in polluted rags, for heav'n unfit,
To sink into the dismal shades of hell!

Where's then the spotless robe in which, array'd,
The happy soul may from the righteous Judge
Meet an eternal smile, and sit approv'd
In that august assembly, where the man
In all the Godhead cloth'd presides supreme?
Not that *self-wrought*, by Pharisees of old
Held in such high esteem—the piercing eye
Of Him who sits on his eternal throne
Thro' the appearance searches to the heart,
And, short of what springs thence in genuine streams
Of pure affection, and obedience pure,
No works can in his sight acceptance find:
But human nature and perfection now
Meet not on earth—heav'n is their meeting-place,
And *Christ* their Centre—from his fulness flows
All that can render human nature fair
In God's all-searching eye. On earth he wrought
A robe of righteousness, which covers all
The sins of his elect; and now in heav'n
He sits an Advocate to plead their cause!
His merit and his sufferings of their hope
Are all the ground, the firm foundation, where

The

The heav'n-taught-wife build for eternity.
This is the robe in which the saints shall stand
Before the great tribunal, from the law,
With all its threat'nings, freely justify'd,
When rolling years, and months, and weeks, and days,
And cold, and heat, and changing light and shade,
With all the marks and measurements of time,
Give place to one eternal blaze of day!

THE FLOWER.

LOVE is the sweetest bud that blows,
   Its beauty never dies;
On earth among the saints it grows,
   And ripens in the skies.

Pure, glowing, red, and spotless white,
   Its perfect colours are;
In Jesus all its sweets unite,
   And look divinely fair.

The finest flow'r that ever blow'd
   Open'd on Calv'ry's tree
When Jesu's blood in rivers flow'd
   For love of worthless me!

Its deepest hue, its richest smell,
   No mortal sense can bear;
Nor can the tongue of angels tell
   How bright the colours are.

Earth could not hold so rich a flow'r,
    Nor half its beauties shew;
Nor could the world and satan's pow'r
    Confine its sweets below.

On Canaan's banks, supremely fair,
    This flow'r of wonders blooms;
Transplanted to its native air,
    And all the shores perfumes.

But, not to Canaan's shores confin'd,
    The seeds which from it blow
Take root within the human mind,
    And scent the church below.

And soon on yonder banks above
    Shall every blossom here
Appear a full-ripe flow'r of love,
    Like Him, transplanted there.

Oh what a garden will be seen
    When all the flow'rs of grace
Appear in everlasting green
    Before the Planter's face!

No more expos'd to burning skies,
    Or winter's piercing cold;
What never-dying sweets will rise
    From every op'ning fold!

No want of sun or show'rs above
  To make the flow'rs decline;
Fountains of life and beams of love
  For ever spring and shine.

No more they need the quick'ning air,
  Or gently falling dew;
Unspeakable their beauties are,
  And yet for ever new.

Christ is their shade, and Christ their sun;
  Among them walks the KING;
Whose presence is ETERNAL NOON,
  His smiles ETERNAL SPRING.

ON PSALM XXIV.

LIFT up your heads, ye gates,
  Your golden hinges move;
The King of glory waits—
  Admit the God of love!
Your everlasting arches raise,
And, as he enters, shout his praise.

Who is this glorious King,
  Who at the portal stands?
What title does he bring,
  That he access demands?
Jehovah's name, in battle strong,
Demands access, inspires the song.

Lift up your heads, ye gates;
　Ye heav'ns, expand your doors;
The King of glory waits
　To spread your golden floors
With spoils thro' death and darkness borne,
With trophies from destruction torn.

Who is this glorious King?
　The Lord that built the skies:
His praise the seraphs sing,
　The holy, just, and wise:
Creation rose at his command,
Redemption owns his sov'reign hand.

The pow'rs of hell oppos'd,
　While he in conflict bled;
And death's strong bars were clos'd
　Round his expiring head:
But death and hell possest no pow'r
To hold him past th' appointed hour.

The hour appointed came,
　The God put off the clay;
And, like a rapid flame,
　Burst through them all his way:
A way so wide, so unconfin'd,
That all his church might march behind.

Lift

Lift your immortal heads,
   Your Lord's from conquest come;
On death and sin he treads;
   Let heav'n prepare him room:
A sheaf of glory's harvest-ears *
The Victor in his chariot bears!

CHRIST THE WAY TO GOD.

JESUS, how heav'nly is the place
   Where thy dear people wait for thee!
Where the rich fountain of thy grace
   Stands ever open, full and free.

Hungry, and poor, and lame, and blind,
   Hither thy blood-bought children fly;
In thy deep wounds a balsam find,
   And live, while they behold thee die.

Here they forget their doubts and fears,
   While thy sharp sorrows meet their eyes;
And bless the hand that dries their tears,
   And with his own their grief supplies.

Oh, the vast myst'ries of thy love!
   How high, how deep, how wide, it rolls!
Its fountain springs in heav'n above,
   Its streams revive our drooping souls!

---

* Alluding to the saints which came out of their graves after his resurrection.

Great was the price to justice due
    When Jesus would redeem his bride;
Nothing but precious blood would do,
    And that must flow from his own side.

Yet from the heights of bliss he fled
    On wings of everlasting love,
And groan'd, and sigh'd, and wept, and bled,
    The mountains of our guilt to move.

How glorious was the work he wrought
    While dwelling in this earthly globe,
When each good deed and each pure thought
    A shuttle prov'd to weave our robe!

Dress'd in this robe, wash'd in this blood,
    And ransom'd from the pow'r of hell,
We now have free access to God,
    And justice likes the payment well.

Thus Jesus wrought our righteousness,
    Our guilt sustain'd, our sorrows bore;
Secur'd our everlasting peace,
    And triumph'd o'er the serpent's pow'r.

And now in heav'n he lives to plead
    Before his holy Father's throne
What he has suffer'd in our stead;
    And sends us gifts and graces down.

And soon will this dear Saviour come,
  In majesty and glory drest,
And take his ransom'd children home
  To seats of everlasting rest.

ON FAITH.

LEAST understood of all the human mind
Has ever exercis'd, and least possest
Of all the graces which adorn the soul—
Bright FAITH, I sing of thee.—So little known
Are thy rare beauties, that wise men have thought
(As this world counts of wisdom) thou hast none.
For they thy name have heard, and wander'd far
To seek thee out, through all the winding ways
That human reason teaches, but in vain;
For thou art from above, they from beneath;
God is thy centre—sinful self is theirs;
Love is thy element, and heav'n the prize
At which thy active hand and piercing eye
Incessant aim.—The world and its delights
(From heav'n abstracted) with magnetic pow'r
Draw them away so far from thy abode,
That they can never meet thee, till their hearts,
Chang'd by almighty grace, admit thy rays,
Thy charms discover, and by thee ascend
To God, whom they without thee cannot please.
By grace divine, the grand efficient cause,

Through faith, the active principle of grace,
Are helpless sinners sav'd. Faith is a plant
Which never grows in nature's barren soil;
Its precious seed from Paradise descends
On the propitious gale of sov'reign love:
Nor is it sown by man—blessings divine
Divinity alone communicates.
Faith comes by hearing, hearing by the word;
Man may dispense the word of God abroad,
But God himself directs it where to fall,
And by his mighty pow'r the heart prepares
First to receive, and then the gift employ.
Faith sees the danger of the human state,
Expos'd by sin to the tremendous curse
Of an infringed law; and Faith perceives,
By revelation's light, the remedy
Of God's appointment in the blood of Christ.
Faith has an eye to pierce the deep obscure
Which rolls between eternity and time,
While yet on shore of time.—Down the steep cliffs
Which overhang that ocean Faith can look
With stedfast eye, nor shudder at the sight.
That awful day, when all the works of man,
Brought to the scale of equity supreme,
Must meet their due from an unerring Judge,
Is ever present in the eye of Faith;
Nor are the gates of glory shut so close
From her approach, but she can sometimes look

Thro' the bright avenues of truth divine,
Behold what paſſes there, and join on earth
The ſhouts of its divine inhabitants!
Faith has an ear to hear the ſtill ſmall voice
Of God the Spirit, which the world around,
Inconſcious of, deny: nor only hears,
But on the wings of ſwift obedience flies
To duty, and in duty finds delight.
Be this, ye ſaints, your work, as ye go on
To your inheritance beyond the grave—
With active underſtanding to explore,
And with delight your Father's will perform.
Faith ſeeks no witneſs to the word of God,
But God the Holy Spirit's ſealing pow'r.
The mind, thereon reclining, ſafely ſleeps,
And wakes ſerenely confident in God:
Thereon depending, all the active ſoul
Againſt the menace of oppoſing hoſts
Undaunted dares advance. What enemy
Can, by ſurpriſe or ſtorm, the ſoul o'ercome
Wall'd by Omnipotence? No courage ſtands
In conflict like the courage built by Faith
On God's immutable eternal love.
Faith in all ages has done wondrous things.—
Abel by Faith excell'd his brother Cain,
When each his offering to Jehovah brought:
By Faith old Enoch ſcal'd the walls of death,
And enter'd heav'n complete, without a wound

From

From his destructive arrows; enter'd heav'n
Triumphant in his great Redeemer's name!
Noah by Faith prepar'd himself an ark,
And weather'd out the storm which sunk a world:
The friend of God, and father of the saints,
Excell'd all others by superior Faith;
And left his name, thus honour'd, on the page
Of Fame's best records to adorn the world:
By Faith the patriarchs thro' this wilderness
Each other follow'd where Jehovah call'd;
Obtain'd at length the Canaan they desir'd,
And won such laurels as will never fade:
By Faith the righteous kings of Israel
Went forth to certain conquest, and return'd
Laden with spoils from slaughter'd enemies,
Ascribing victory to God alone:
One chas'd a thousand, and ten thousand fled
Before two heroes arm'd with Faith divine *!
By Faith the martyrs calmly met the flames
On which to heav'n they rode; unshaken saw
The cruel racks their persecutors brought,
And pray'd for those who us'd them, while they bore
The sharpest torments malice could invent;
Thus arm'd, they smil'd at Persecution's frown,
And wore those laurels with triumphal shouts
Which sprung from ground they water'd with their blood!

* 1 Sam. xiv. 6, &c.

Women, by Faith in Jesus, undismay'd,
Stood firm against the rage of earth and hell
United, and with placid patience bore
The worst extremes of torture and disgrace.
Nor is Faith barren or inactive now,
Tho' now no more the dreadful roar we hear
Of Persecution raging thro' our streets;
The world and Satan still find work to do
For those whose hearts on heavenly things are set:
Without are snares, within depravity,
Which makes the Christian sigh when he would sing;
But, while the conflict lasts, with skill divine
And with divine activity inspir'd,
Faith, like a bee, through all the sacred word
From one sweet promise to another flies,
And sucks from each immortal nourishment;
Till on the rose of Sharon it alights,
(That glorious flow'r which bloom'd on Calvary;
A flow'r whose fragrance fill'd the courts of heav'n
With everlasting sweets, and scented earth
With odours which attract celestial feet):
Then all the passions, overwhelm'd in sweets,
And struck with beauties infinite, dissolve
Into delight serene and rapture strong,
And love and adoration fill the soul!
This was the fight which angels long'd to see,
Which Heav'n look'd down with wonder to behold!
Jehovah's attributes in harmony,

The

The dreadful and the kind, were here display'd;
The Power, the Truth, the Justice, and the Love!
And sinners' names were thro' the scene inscrib'd,
Without their sins annex'd. A spotless host,
Cleans'd from defilement and from guilt set free,
Were in this mirror of perfection seen.
Here towering Faith and her twin-sister Hope
Are born at once, and hand in hand go on
Believing and expecting, till in heaven
The bud becomes a flow'r, the dawn full day,
And both are swallow'd up of perfect LOVE!

ON HOPE.

TIR'D with the retrospect of pleasures past,
And fearing present pleasures may not last,
I call an heav'n-born beauty to my aid,
And court acquaintance with the virtuous maid;
HOPE is her name.—In ever-green array
She walks the day, and waits the night away;
Heav'n is her birth-place, but on earth she lives,
And, by her smiles, the aching heart relieves.
How much may be sustain'd of present ill,
While future prospects keep the passions still!
Hope, from the prison of distress, may see
The mansions of triumphant liberty;
And point the soul, that sits in sorrow's cave,
To pleasures which survive the threat'ning grave;

Alleviating

Alleviating thus it's present pain
By the rich prospect of eternal gain!
Calm in the midst of the surrounding storm,
And in the calmest scene devoutly warm,
Hope, on her anchor leaning, stands secure;
Her ground immutable, her harvest sure!
Such is the Christian's hope;—but hopes there are
Which lead to disappointment and despair;
Founded on quicksands which must soon give way,
And sink the soul that trusts them in dismay.
BEHOLD yon ship by dreadful tempests hurl'd,
From wave to wave, along the wat'ry world;
Now deep beneath the swelling surge it lies,
And now the billows lift it to the skies;
The sailors ply their utmost skill and strength,
And struggle with destruction—till at length,
Worn out with fruitless toil, the helpless crew
Sink in despair, with only death in view!
Now o'er their heads the parting clouds display
A speck of azure, and a glimpse of day;
Swift, as that light darts thro' the gloomy air,
Fair Hope descends, and banishes despair.
To men like these, how welcome such a sight!
Their eyes how glad to meet long absent light!
How does the cheering passion kindle round,
And thankful shouts along the deep resound!
But see a soul, on seas of guilty fear,
From Hope's green shores fast failing for despair!

Unwilling

Unwilling to advance, yet forc'd away
By the strong gale of God's strict equity!
A broken law demands the sinner's blood;
Justice stands plaintiff for an injur'd God;
Conscience, subpœna'd to the awful bar,
Turns evidence, and leaves him to despair!
Condemn'd already, ere his cause is try'd,
Unable Truth's bright presence to abide,
Away he flies!—But whither can he go—
Justice behind, before him endless woe?
Fast to the deep he speeds that leads to hell,
And quits the shores where Hope and Mercy dwell:
Hide me, he cries, from that tremendous frown!
Ye gloomy pow'rs of darkness, drag me down;
And in your closest caverns let me lie
Conceal'd awhile from that all-searching eye!
Now on the verge of time behold him stand,
Behind pursu'd, beset on either hand;
The shoreless ocean of eternity,
As he advances, gaining on his eye:
Billows of endless fire around him roll,
And bursting thunders shake his guilty soul!
Now where is Hope? Can God or Justice change?
Can hell be quench'd, or souls immortal range
A circuit wider than Jehovah's eye,
And thus avoid eternal misery?
No!—God's immutable,—and Justice hears
No suppliant's cry, is melted by no tears;

Not penitence itself has pow'r to ward
The guilty foul from his avenging sword,
Nor can a creature from Jehovah's eye
Be hid one moment of eternity!
Yet, lo, superior to this tenfold night,
Fair Hope appears in robes of heavenly light!
From her bright lamp almighty Mercy beams!
Where shines this prodigy?——
                    From Sinai's flames
And hell's deep caverns turn away thine eyes,
And see on Calvary the Day-star rise!
Jesus the SAVIOUR has atonement made!
Jesus the SURETY all the debt has paid!
Jesus the MAN restores the broken law!
Justice from sinners may his hand withdraw;
Jesus the GOD gives sanction to the deed,
And Truth herself proclaims the sinner freed!
This is the ground where HOPE OF GLORY
         stands,
And boundless prospects of delight commands;
This is the way, and this the only road,
From sin and death to holiness and God:
All other paths to hopeless ruin tend,
And must at length in hopeless ruin end.
Jehovah's name in JESUS is reveal'd;
Behind his common works it lies conceal'd.
Search Nature's volume through, and thou shalt see
In ev'ry flower, and plant, and bush, and tree,
                              The

The footsteps of a God are left behind;
But God himself in these thou canst not find.
Or lift thine eyes, and thro' the trackless air
Inquire his name of ev'ry rolling star;
Ask them who gave their lucid substance birth,
And taught their wondrous influence on the earth:
They'll tell thee all, as in their spheres they shine,
Their lustre's borrow'd from a boundless mine;
God they proclaim to all the creatures round,
From Albion's shores to earth's remotest bound;
But what his name, his nature, or his will,
Their silent beams in darkness leave thee still.
His name's a secret thou canst never know
From ought above the stars or ought below,
Till through thy heart he makes each letter shine
In crimson characters of blood divine.
God is the ocean of delight unknown,
That fills the happy myriads round his throne!
Grace from this ocean like a river rose,
And back to God with ceaseless motion flows.
Mercy's fair vessel on this river sails
Safe to the port of heav'n, nor ever fails.
No storms can sink the soul that ventures here,
This Hope was never conquer'd by despair:
This is the stable anchor of the soul,
That fix'd abides while tempests round it roll;
Long is the cable, but it's hold is sure,
The saints shall triumph, but they must endure.

THE WELLS OF SALVATION.

WHAT joys unspeakable are felt and sung
When Christians round Salvation's living wells
Exulting stand, and wonder at the love
Which burst the fountains open! Love immense—
An ocean without bounds! Jehovah's love,
Unsought by sinners, yet to sinners flows
Free as the air they breathe into their lips!
How does a drop increase into a stream
In every heart that feels it, and a stream
As fast into a flowing river rise!
Where stands this fountain? Calvary's the spot.—
Not that which pilgrims visit in the land
Which once was holy, where Emmanuel dy'd;
Unholy feet may climb that horrid steep,
And walk unholy down: no virtue there
To cleanse or to refresh was ever found.
This sacred hill, whence life's eternal spring
Incessant flows, is holy, heav'nly ground;
And Faith alone the steep ascent can climb.
Yet such the virtue of this fountain is,
That only Faith can taste it—living faith
In a once dead Redeemer—living faith
In him who dy'd, but now for ever lives;
And lives to the same end for which he dy'd!
Faith of old time turn'd rivers into blood,

And

And thus evinc'd its origin divine;
And thus the King of kings was glorify'd
In the deftruction of a rebel realm.
Now faith divine, with fkill divinely taught,
Draws living water from redeeming blood;—
That well without a bottom, ftill fupply'd
From the vaft fea of everlafting love.
Pure is this water, and the foul that drinks
Is by it purify'd; nothing unclean,
Approaching it, returns unclean away.
Here, finner, thy polluted foul immerfe:
And, though the guilt of fin original,
And fins committed, fink thee down to hell
In expectation. On the wings of faith
To heav'n from this pure fountain thou fhalt rife
And find admittance there; the op'ning gates
Shall found thy welcome, as their leaves expand:
The facred bofom of redeeming Love
Shall give thee entrance into reft fupreme;
While fov'reign Mercy's everlafting arms
Clafp thee with love parental, and proclaim
Thy fonfhip to the bleft inhabitants:
The bleft inhabitants, with fhouts fublime,
Shall fing of thy falvation, till the fhouts
Fly over all the everlafting hills,
And vaft eternity replies, Amen.
This fountain, when the weary traveller,
On pilgrimage to Zion, faint with thirft,

Approaches

Approaches for refreshment, yields him strength
Immediate, and his weary soul renews
So sudden, that he soon, if walking, runs;
And, if he ran before, takes wing and flies
Like a young eagle * to the gates of heav'n.

WHAT MUST WE DO TO BE JOYFUL?

REJOICE in God, the word commands,
   And feign would I obey;
Yet still my ling'ring spirit stands
   And trembles with delay.

How can my soul exult for joy
   Which feels this load of sin?
How can sweet praise my tongue employ
   While darkness reigns within?

Whence should my lips give rapture birth,
   When I no rapture feel?
Or how should notes of heav'nly mirth
   Sound from an heart of steel?

If falling tears and rising sighs
   In triumph share a part;
Then, Lord, behold these streaming eyes,
   And search this bleeding heart.

* Isaiah xl. 31.

My foul forgets to ufe her wings;
    My harp neglected lies;
For fin has broken all its ftrings,
    And guilt fhuts out my joys.

In vain I fearch the creatures round;
    Their ev'ry anfwer this—
" No pleafure can in us be found
    If God is not your blifs."

At length I hear a gentle voice
    Salute my ravifh'd ears—
" Rejoice, thou ranfom'd foul, rejoice,
    And dry thofe falling tears!

Amaz'd, I turn, grown ftrangely bold,
    This wond'rous thing to fee;
And there my dying Lord behold,
    Stretch'd on the bloody tree!

" Sinner," he cries, " behold the head
    This thorny wreath entwines;
Look on thefe wounded hands, and read
    Thy name in crimfon lines :

Thefe wounds I bear, thefe pains I feel,
    This anguifh rends my breaft,
That I may fave thy foul from hell,
    And give thee endlefs reft,"

The pow'r, the sweetness, of that voice
   My stony heart can move,
Make me in Christ my Lord rejoice,
   And melt my soul to love.

No more my harp neglected lies
   With silent, broken strings;
From earth my soul has learn'd to rise,
   And mounts on eagles' wings.

My dying Saviour's wond'rous love
   On earth employs my tongue;
And when I walk in white above
   That love shall be my song.

PRAISE FOR SALVATION.

FATHER, our hearts would now aspire,
On wings of faith and strong desire,
'To thy celestial courts above,
Where all is glory, peace, and love.

We praise thee for the boundless grace
Extended to our fallen race,
When we, in our first parents, fell
From Eden to the gates of hell.

We praise the Son, who freely came
From heav'n to bear our sin and shame;
Who fought, who conquer'd, all our foes,
And bore the weight of all our woes.

We bless the Spirit's sacred name,
Who kindled that internal flame
Of holy faith, and holy love,
Which draws and keeps our hearts above.

PRAISE FOR A COMPLETE SAVIOUR.

WE long for that fair morning's light,
When we, in robes of spotless white,
Shall join the bright redeemed throng
To sing that new and endless song—

To him that lov'd us when we lay
Conceal'd in uncreated clay;
To him that lov'd us, though we fell,
And sav'd us from the pains of hell—

To him that found us dead in sin,
And planted holy life within;
To him that taught our feet the way
From endless night to endless day—

To him that wrought our righteousness,
And sanctify'd us by his grace;
To him that brought us back to God,
Thro' the red sea of his own blood—

To him that sits upon the throne,
The great, eternal Three in One—
To him let saints and angels raise
An everlasting song of praise!

A PROSPECT OF THE LAST DAY.

I KNOW that my Redeemer lives:
And that bright morning will appear
When every soul that now believes
Shall rise and meet him in the air.

Soon shall the op'ning clouds disclose
The terrors of the Judge's frown
To all his now presumptuous foes,
And thunder swift destruction down.

The awful trumpet's solemn sound
Shall soon his near approach declare,
And all that sleep beneath the ground
His life-restoring voice shall hear.

What wond'rous grandeur, pow'r, and love,
Will our Redeemer then display,
While earth beneath and heav'n above
At once his potent call obey!

But the same voice that rends the skies,
And hurls the wicked down to hell,
Shall bid the happy saints arise,
And with their Lord in glory dwell.

Triumphant over sin and death,
These bodies into life shall spring;
And tune their first celestial breath
A bleeding Saviour's love to sing.

AD-

ADMIRATION AND JOYFUL EXPECTATION.

AND am I bleft with Jefu's love?
And fhall I dwell with him above?
And will the joyful period come
When I fhall call the heav'ns my home?

Think, O my foul, what muft it be
A world of glorious minds to fee,
Drink at the fountain head of peace,
And bathe in everlafting blifs!

To hear them all at once proclaim
Eternal glories to the Lamb;
And join, with joyful heart and tongue,
That new, that never-ending fong!

And does the happy hour draw near,
When Chrift will in the clouds appear;
And I without a vail fhall fee
The MAN, the GOD that bled for me!

If in my foul fuch joy abounds
While weeping faith explores his wounds,
How glorious will thofe fcars appear
When perfect blifs forbids a tear!

Think, O my foul, if 'tis fo fweet
On earth to fit at Jefu's feet,
What muft it be to wear a crown,
And fit with Jefus on his throne!

THE COMING OF CHRIST TO JUDGMENT.

LO, he comes, array'd in vengeance,
   Riding down the heav'nly road;
Floods of fury roll before him.—
   Who can meet an angry God?
      Tremble sinners,
   Who can stand before his rod!

Lo he comes, in glory shining;
   Saints, arise and meet your King!
" Glorious Captain of salvation,
   Welcome! welcome!" hear them sing!
      Shouts of triumph,
   Make the heav'ns with echoes ring.

Now, despisers, look and wonder!
   Hear the dreadful sound " Depart,"
Rattling, like a peal of thunder,
   Thro' each guilty rebel's heart!
      Lost for ever,
   Hope and sinners here must part!

Still they hear the awful sentence;
   Hell resounds the dreadful roar,
While their heart-strings twinge with anguish,
   Trembling on the burning shore!
      Justice seals it—
   Down they sink, to rise no more!

How they shrink, with horror viewing
   Hell's deep caverns op'ning wide!
Guilty thoughts, like ghosts pursuing,
   Plunge them down the rolling tide!
      Now consider,
Ye who scorn the Lamb that dy'd!

Hark! ten thousand harps resounding!
   Form'd in bright and grand array,
See the glorious armies rising,
   While their Captain leads the way!
      Heav'n before them
Opens an eternal day!

COMMUNION WITH SAINTS ABOVE.

'TIS good to wait upon the Lord
   When Christ himself draws near,
And ev'ry heart with one accord
   Ascends in solemn prayer.

While thus we feel the Saviour's love
   In heav'nly show'rs descend,
Our souls commune with saints above
   In bliss that knows no end.

We taste the precious streams of grace;
   The fountain makes them sing:
We travel thro' the wilderness;
   They sit before the King.

We pray for grace to hold out well
  The conflict but begun;
They of their past engagements tell,
  And sing the conquests won.

We fight the battles of the Lord,
  And are sometimes cast down;
They wield no more the warrior's sword,
  But wear the conqueror's crown.

The saints above, in spotless white,
  For ever sing and shine;
Our clothing oft abhors the light,
  And we in darkness pine.

Yet we all eat one living bread,
  And share one noble birth;
Tho' they in heav'n are richly fed,
  And we supply'd on earth.

They all were once as vile as we,
  And wore the chains of sin;
Like us they struggled to be free,
  And mourn'd the plague within.

And soon shall we, as bright as they,
  In robes of honour shine,
And spend with them an endless day,
  In pleasures all divine.

Then

Then shall we all begin at home
   One everlasting song:
Till then, dear Lord, thy kingdom come!
   Nor let the time be long.

A PROSPECT OF THE RESURRECTION.

WHAT joys will crown that happy hour,
When in the air the Lord we meet,
And triumph o'er infernal pow'r,
With Satan bruis'd beneath our feet!

When waking millions burst their way,
Invested with immortal white,
And freed from chains of mould'ring clay,
Thro' death's strong bars to op'ning light!

When happy myriads with their Lord
Descend betwixt the op'ning skies,
And fly, at his almighty word,
To meet their bodies as they rise.

Then we, who feel guilt's barbed sting,
And sin's pernicious influence prove,
Shall, with the rising armies, sing
The wonders of redeeming love!

Then shall the broken wheels of time
To vast eternity give way;
While we ascend the heav'nly clime,
To spend an everlasting day.

No sin shall in our hearts abide;
No pining wish, no anxious care,
No secret lust, no swelling pride,
No thought but love, shall harbour there.

In that bright world no cloud shall rise
To wrap the heav'nly scenes in night;
No darkness vail th' eternal skies,
Or shade their everlasting light.

CHRISTIAN ENCOURAGEMENT.

TEMPTED souls, arise and sing;
Conquest soon your heads shall crown,
Jesus, our victorious King,
Soon shall tread the tempter down.

Soon before your joyful eyes
Satan shall in chains appear,
Sentenc'd (never more to rise)
To the realms of dark despair.

Weeping saints, a little while
Banish'd from the light of day,
Soon before your Saviour's smile
Every shade will fly away.

Clouds may thro' the night endure,
But the morning soon will come,
When, from future clouds secure,
Zion's sun shall light you home.

Happy

Happy souls, who read your names
In your Saviour's bleeding wounds,
While your love ascends in flames,
While your faith and hope abounds,

Shout his praises more and more;
Tell the world a Saviour's love,
Till that Saviour you adore
In the happy world above!

PRAISE FOR REDEEMING LOVE.

HOSANNA to the God of love,
Who condescended from above
   To bring salvation down!
We bless his name, who stoop'd so low
To save us from eternal woe,
   And raise us to a crown.

When we, in our first parents, fell
From Eden to the gates of hell,
   And lay like captives there,
Then Jesus cast a pitying eye
On wretches doom'd for sin to lie
   For ever in despair.

His bowels, where compassion rolls,
Then yearning o'er our guilty souls,

Did first for sinners move.
His op'ning heart display'd our names,
And issu'd forth in quenchless flames
   Of everlasting love.

His majesty he laid aside,
Obedient liv'd, submissive dy'd,
   Our ruin'd souls to save.
The pow'rs of hell he trampled down,
But sunk, beneath his Father's frown,
   From Calv'ry to the grave.

How vast the sufferings who can tell,
When Jesus fought sin, death, and hell,
   And was in battle slain?
How great the triumph who can sing,
When from the grave th' immortal King
   Triumphant rose again?

Yet we'll attempt his name to bless
While we pass thro' the wilderness
   To Canaan's happy shore.
But when we reach the plains above,
And every breath we draw is love,
   We'll sing his glories more.

A RESPONSIVE HYMN.

MEN.

LIFT up your hearts in solemn lays,
Ye daughters of the heav'nly King.

WOMEN.

Our hearts we lift, our songs we raise;
And Jesus is the theme we sing!

MEN.

Jesus! the glorious name revives
Our drooping hearts when troubles rise.

WOMEN.

In him the strength of Zion lives;
By him the pow'r of Satan dies.

MEN.

'Twas he who hung upon the tree
With pierced hands and wounded side.

WOMEN.

Believing soul, he bled for thee;
For thee the King of glory dy'd!

MEN.

For us he dy'd, for us he rose;
To us, in him, are all things giv'n:

WOMEN.

His own right-arm subdu'd our foes;
And now he reigns for us in heav'n.

BOTH

BOTH.

His bosom is the fountain head,
Which flows with everlasting love.
Join every tongue his praise to spread,
Whose praise employs the hosts above.

THE GRACE OF CHRISTIAN LOVE.

HOW sweet, how heav'nly is the sight,
 When those that love the Lord
In one another's peace delight,
 And so fulfil his word.

When each can feel his brother sigh,
 And with him bear a part;
When sorrow flows from eye to eye,
 And joy from heart to heart.

When, free from envy, scorn, and pride,
 Our wishes all above,
Each can his brother's failings hide,
 And shew a brother's love.

When love, in one delightful stream,
 Thro' every bosom flows;
When union sweet, and dear esteem,
 In every action glows.

Love is the golden chain that binds
 The happy souls above;
And he's an heir of heav'n that finds
 His bosom glow with love.

CHRIST

CHRIST THE ONLY REFUGE FOR LOST SINNERS.

SINNERS, away from Sinai fly!
To Calv'ry's bloody scene repair;
Behold the Prince of glory die,
And read your dear-bought pardon there!

Search into every open wound;
Trace the sharp scourge, the nails, the spear;
And thy salvation will be found
In golden letters written there.

No works of man, to raise the sum
Or pay the ransom, must be brought;
Helpless and poor to Jesus come,
Nor strive to bring a perfect thought.

Your faith, your hope, and righteousness,
Are treasur'd up in him alone;
Your rich supplies of grace and peace
Spring from the works your Lord has done.

Hell opens her ten thousand graves
To swallow those that die in sin;
But all the great Emmanuel saves
Heav'ns open gates shall welcome in.

There shall the blood-wash'd armies go
That trust the great Redeemer here;
The plant that buds with grace below
Shall ripen into glory there!

A SOUL MELTED WITH REDEEMING LOVE.

WHEN on my beloved I gaze,
So dazzling his beauties appear,
His charms so transcendantly blaze,
The sight is too melting to bear!

When from my own vileness I turn
To Jesus, expos'd on the tree,
With shame and with wonder I burn,
To think what he suffer'd for me.

My sins, oh how black they appear,
When in that dear bosom they meet!
Those sins were the nails and the spear
That wounded his hands and his feet.

'Twas Justice that wreath'd for his head
The thorns that encircled it round.
Thy temples, Emmanuel, bled,
That mine might with glory be crown'd!

The wonderful love of his heart,
Where he has recorded my name,
On earth can be known but in part,
Heaven only can bear the full flame.

In rivers of sorrow it flow'd,
And flow'd in those rivers for me;
My sins are all drown'd in his blood;
My soul is both happy and free.

SECOND

SECOND PART.

HOW willing was Jesus to die,
That we, fellow sinners, might live!
The life they could not take away
How ready was Jesus to give!

They pierced his hands and his feet;
His hands and his feet he resign'd;
The pangs of his body were great,
But greater the pangs of his mind.

That wrath would have kindled a hell
Of never-abating despair
In millions of creatures, which fell
On Jesus, and spent itself there.

Divinity burst in a blaze
Of vengeance on Jesus our head;
Divinity's indwelling rays
Sustain'd him till nature was dead.

Divinity back to his frame
The life he had yielded restor'd,
And Jesus, entomb'd, was the same
With Jesus in glory ador'd.

No nearer we venture than this,
To gaze on a deep so profound;
But tread, while we taste of the bliss,
With reverence the hallow'd ground.

THE CHRISTIAN's COMPANY AND EMPLOYMENT.

JESUS, away from earth I fly,
   And with thy church unite;
Thy saints shall be my company,
   Thy presence my delight.

Thy name shall dwell upon my tongue,
   Thro' all the heav'nly road;
Thy truth and grace shall be my song
   Till I get home to God.

The wonders of thy bleeding love
   For one so vile as I
Shall often draw my heart above,
   And fix my thoughts on high.

Yes, in thy name I will rejoice,
   And triumph in thy word;
In echo to my heart, my voice
   Shall magnify the Lord.

And may I never cease to tell
   The wonders of his love,
Till heav'nly notes my bosom swell
   In yonder courts above:

Till I, without a jarring sound,
   Thy free salvation sing,
And make those chrystal walls resound
   The glories of my King.

THE CONVERSION OF A SINNER.

ON the brink of fiery ruin
    Juſtice, with a flaming ſword,
Was my guilty ſoul purſuing,
    When I firſt beheld my Lord.

Terrify'd with Sinai's thunder,
    Straight I flew to Calvary;
Where I ſaw with love and wonder
    Him, by faith, who dy'd for me.

" Sinner," he exclaim'd, " I've lov'd thee
    With an everlaſting love;
Juſtice has in me approv'd thee,
    Thou ſhalt dwell with me above."

Sweet as angels' notes in heav'n,
    When to golden harps they ſound,
Is the voice of ſins forgiv'n
    To the ſoul by Satan bound:

Sweet as angels' harps in glory
    Was that heav'nly voice to me,
When I ſaw my Lord, before me,
    Bleed and die to ſet me free!

Saints, attend with holy wonder!
    Sinners, hear and ſing his praiſe!
'Tis the God that holds the thunder
    Shews himſelf the God of grace!

AN ENCOURAGING PROSPECT FOR BELIEVERS.

EXALT, ye saints, the Lord your King,
    While time inceſſant moves:
Chriſtians of grace ſhould always ſing,
    For Jeſus always loves.

Swift as the winged moments roll
    Our feet to Canaan move;
And ſoon ſhall each enraptur'd ſoul
    Be ſwallow'd up in love.

Soon ſhall the heav'nly gates unfold
    To us their pearly leaves,
And we ſhall with theſe eyes behold
    What now our faith believes.

There ſhall our diſembody'd ſouls
    With all they ſeek be bleſs'd;
And bathe, till time no longer rolls,
    In undiſturbed reſt:

Then with our glorious Lord deſcend
    Betwixt the op'ning ſkies,
And hear his voice the mountains rend,
    And ſee the dead ariſe.

And (while in flames the wicked burn)
    With bodies heav'nly fair,
Home with our Jeſus we'll return,
    And ſing his praiſes there.

THE SOUL RESISTING TEMPTATIONS.

LORD, at thy feet in duſt I lie,
   Nor can from thence remove;
If I muſt periſh—here I'll die,
   Depending on thy love.

I'll ſing redeeming grace in hell,
   If ever I go there;
Of Jeſu's wounds and paſſion tell,
   While devils howl deſpair.

I plead no merits of my own,
   I've trampled on thy laws;
Thy Juſtice, Lord, might ſtrike me dead,
   But Jeſus pleads my cauſe.

On him I caſt my helpleſs ſoul,
   Nor Satan's malice fear;
Tho' hell's black waves againſt me roll,
   I'll ſeek my refuge there.

I'll look into his wounded ſide,
   Whence all my comforts flow;
Nor ſhall my ſoul be ſatisfy'd
   Till I my int'reſt know.

I'll plead and pray, and never ceaſe
   While Jeſus lives in heav'n,
Till he ſhall bid me go in peace,
   And ſhew my ſins forgiv'n.

Then, in the face of hell and death,
    In weakness more than strong,
Salvation shall employ my breath,
    And grace be all my song.

Yea, tho' ten thousand foes I meet,
    Onward I still will go;
His love shall make my trials sweet,
    His grace shall bring me through:

Till I arrive on Canaan's shore,
    With all the saints above,
Never to sin or sorrow more,
    But sing, and praise, and love.

HOLY CONFIDENCE.

WHEN firm I stand on Zion's hill,
    And view my starry crown,
No pow'r on earth my hope can shake,
    Nor hell can pluck me down.

The lofty hills and stately tow'rs,
    That lift their heads so high,
Shall all be levell'd in the dust;
    Their very names shall die.

The vaulted heav'ns shall melt away,
    Built by Jehovah's hands;
But firmer than the heav'ns the rock
    Of my salvation stands.

THE COMING OF CHRIST ANTICIPATED.

COME, lift your joyous eyes
  To yonder heav'nly place,
Where, freed from fin, your fouls fhall rife,
  And fing redeeming grace.

Tho' death and hell may frown,
  And charge the faints with guilt;
Yet death and hell fhall ne'er pull down
  The church which Chrift has built.

To Sion's blifsful fhore,
  As on our way we go,
While hallelujahs found before,
  'Tis heav'n begun below.

Then caft your willows down;
  Lift up your hearts and fing,
Till Chrift your heads with glory crown,
  And make each faint a king.

In expectation fweet
  We'll wait, and fing, and pray,
Till his triumphal car we meet,
  And fee an endlefs day.

He comes! he comes! behold
  His prefence melts the fky!
Celeftial armies, clad in gold,
  Around his chariot fly.

He comes! the conqu'ror comes!
Death falls beneath his sword;
The joyful pris'ners burst the tombs,
And rise to meet their Lord!

The trumpet sounds, "Awake!—
Ye dead, to judgment come!"
The pillars of creation shake
While hell receives her doom.

Thrice happy morn for those
Who love the ways of peace;
No night of sorrow e'er shall close,
Or shade, their perfect bliss.

NEW COVENANT JOY.

REJOICE, ye saints of God,
Whose undiverted feet
Still travel Zion's road
Your gracious Lord to meet;
Whose bosoms glow with holy love,
Whose hearts and hopes are fix'd above.

We are not come to gaze
On Sinai's mount with awe,
Or meet the angry blaze
Of God's indignant law,
While round us flames of wrath divine
In all their dreadful glories shine;

We are not come to hear
The thunder of that word
That fills the soul with fear,
And leaves the heart still hard;
That sends the trembling wretch away
Without a glimpse of heav'nly day.

But we are come to hear
The sound of gospel peace,
That scatters slavish fear,
And kindles hopes of bliss;
That shews our wand'ring feet the way
From darkness to eternal day:

But we are come to meet
The smiles of love divine,
From off the mercy's seat,
Where milder glories shine;
Where God the Father waits to hear
The vilest sinner's humble pray'r:

Where Jesus, our high-priest,
A mediator stands,
And wears the sacred vest;
And fills his holy hands
With his vicarious sacrifice,
Thro' which our pray'rs accepted rise,

Thence

Thence he the Spirit sends
Like a celestial dove,
To crown his earthly friends
With honours from above;
To teach the sinners how to pray,
And guide the saints in Zion's way.

Yes, we are come to join
The bright assembled throng
That, wash'd in blood divine,
Exalt th' angelic song;
That glory in the Saviour's name,
And sing the sin-atoning Lamb.

On earth the song begins,
In heav'n more sweet and loud,
To him that drowns our sins
In his atoning blood;
To him they cry, in rapt'rous strain,
" Be honour, praise, and pow'r. Amen!"

Ye saints, on earth, repeat
What heav'n with rapture owns;
And while before his feet
The elders cast their crowns,
Go imitate the choirs above,
And tell the world your Saviour's love.

Sing as ye paſs along,
With joy and wonder ſing,
Till ſinners catch the ſong,
And own your Lord their King;
Till converts join you as ye go,
And make a growing heav'n below.

Inform the liſt'ning world
How Jeſus, when he fell,
The pow'rs of darkneſs hurl'd
Down to the deeps of hell;
And, riſing, bore the reſcu'd prize,
His church, in triumph thro' the ſkies.

Alone he took the field,
Alone the battle fought;
With his own ſword and ſhield
The mighty work he wrought.
The mighty work was all his own,
And let him ever wear the crown.

From heav'n, on wings of love,
The kind Deliv'rer came,
And left the joys above
To bear our ſin and ſhame.
No hand but thine ſuch work could do!
No heart but thine ſuch love could ſhew!

How bright thy glories shine,
Redeemer of our race;
Thy honours are divine,
Divine thy sov'reign grace!
The grace that tunes our mortal tongues
To sound the notes which heav'n prolongs!

Our feeble minds are lost
Beneath the lofty strain;
But, Jordan's billows croft,
We'll catch the sound again;
In praise assist th' angelic choir,
Nor ever stop, nor ever tire.

THE COURAGE OF FAITH.

MY soul, unfetter'd by the skies,
Or ought the fruitful earth conceals,
On faith's broad wings to heaven would rise,
The heav'n where my Redeemer dwells.

There, while the Godhead he displays
Thro' human beauty, void of fear,
I'd give my bosom to the blaze
Of every grace that centers there!

Yes, I would call my Jesus mine,
While seraphs " Holy, holy," cry;
And meet the smile of love divine,
Tho' cloth'd in peerless majesty.

THE

THE GIFT OF DIVINE PEACE.

THE peace which thro' the ſtorm
Of time unſhaken lives,
To us unworthy worms
The King of Sion gives;
His princely hand the gift beſtows
Not as the world—but on his foes!

By purchaſe and by pow'r
He bought and took the prize
In one tremendous hour,
And bore it thro' the ſkies;
And now he ſends it freely down
On all who aſk the precious boon.

He makes his foes his friends,
He conquers them by love;
And, with their pardon, ſends
His Spirit from above;
Their peace and pardon ſeal'd with blood,
They run with joy the heav'nly road.

HEAVEN WILL MAKE AMENDS FOR ALL.

WHILE pilgrims on this earthly ball,
Our ſweeteſt joys are ting'd with gall;
The diſtant things, which promiſe reſt,
Prove leſs than nothing when poſſeſt.

Pleaſure,

Pleasure, while we pursue it, flies,
And fancy'd bliss deludes our eyes;
While grace bedews with many a tear
The ground which sin has sown with care.

But in the glorious worlds on high
No sorrows spring, no comforts die;
Immortal pleasures feast the soul,
And joys in endless rivers roll.

No more the cheek turn'd pale with fear,
The rising sigh, the falling tear;
The plaintive soul immers'd no more
In seas of grief without a shore.

Guilt's barbed sting, with piercing smart,
No more shall wound the trembling heart;
Wash'd from our sins in Jesu's blood,
We then shall know the peace of God.

THE FRUITS OF PARDONING GRACE.

LORD, my very heart would bleed,
While for pard'ning love I plead;
When I think what various ways
I've abus'd thy wond'rous grace:

Still I fly to Jesu's veins;
There I wash my guilty stains;
There, from my polluted soul,
All my sins like mountains roll.

Low beneath thy feet I lie;
Let me live, or bid me die;
But, if thou my days prolong,
Shew thyself in weakness strong.

O may ev'ry hour to come
Bring me near my heav'nly home;
Near in life, and near in heart,
Till my soul and sin shall part!

May I, all along the road,
Follow my Redeemer, God;
Ever rising let me be
Till I rise to dwell with thee.

THE DYING LOVE OF CHRIST.

WHEN I by faith my Saviour see,
And think what he has done for me,
It strikes my soul with sweet surprize,
And fills with tears my wond'ring eyes!—
His blood was shed to set me free
From everlasting misery!

On all his beauties while I gaze,
And see them in his suff'rings blaze,
My heart, like wax before the fire,
Melts into love and strong desire.—
His blood was shed to set me free
From everlasting misery!

Was it for me those hands were torn?
For me he suffer'd shame and scorn?
Was it my name which, written there,
Drew to his heart the bloody spear?—
Was his blood shed to set me free
From everlasting misery?

Did Jesus hide me in his veins?
And did my sins awake those pains
Which, like a fire, thro' all his frame
Ravag'd in one devouring flame?—
Was his blood shed to set me free
From everlasting misery?

Why did the Lord in anger frown?
Why did his Father's wrath come down
In storms, to shake his spotless soul,
And through his heart like waters roll?—
Why, but to set poor sinners free
From everlasting misery?

Yes, Jesus did resign his breath,
And suffer'd all the pangs of death,
That we might see his Father's face,
And taste the sweets of pard'ning grace:—
His blood was shed to set us free
From everlasting misery!

With such a Saviour, such a King,
Who can but love! who can but sing!

An Interceffor fo divine
Makes ev'ry face with gladnefs fhine;—
Whofe blood was fhed to fet us free
From everlafting mifery!

THE ASSURANCE OF FAITH.

THE Lord, whofe throne is fix'd on high,
The God of glory and of love,
That treads the clouds beneath his feet,
And rules the wond'rous worlds above:

The God that built the ftarry roof
That over-hangs this fpacious earth,
That laid the floors of heav'n with gold,
And gave the whole creation birth:—

This God is mine, and I am his—
Eternal glory to his name!
Tho' time and nature ftop their courfe,
My God and Saviour is the fame.

Tho' hell and fin, with all their hofts
United, rife my faith to move,
Fix'd on this rock I ftand fecure,
And triumph in redeeming love.

When earth and heav'n fhall roll away,
My foul, beyond the reach of fear,
In a new heav'n fhall meet her Lord,
And reign for ever with him there.

THE PILGRIMS' SONG.

TO Zion we go, the seat of our King,
And yet while below we cannot but sing.
Tho' few here esteem us, the God we adore
Has dy'd to redeem us—what could he do more?

What Jesus has done to save us from hell;
What conquests he won when he himself fell;
The depths of his sorrow, the heights of his love,
Will never be known till we sing them above.

Then trust in his name, and rest on his word;
He's always the same unchangable Lord;
His wisdom's omniscient, his pow'r is supreme,
His grace is sufficient his flock to redeem.

Tho' foes in the way we oftentimes meet,
And Satan will lay fresh snares for our feet,
Our journey to Zion we still will pursue;
The God we rely on is faithful and true.

Tho' we may seem small to those whom we fear,
Yet what are they all when Jesus is near?
His grace and his Spirit for us are employ'd;
His blood and his merit are both on our side.

Then what shall we fear? In life and in death
His Spirit can cheer our hope and our faith:
In sweet expectation we'll wait till he come;
The Lord our salvation will soon fetch us home.

MUTUAL

MUTUAL ENCOURAGEMENT.

BRETHREN, while we sojourn here,
Fight we must, but should not fear;
Foes we have, but we've a friend,
One that loves us to the end.
Forward then with courage go,
Long we shall not dwell below;
Soon the joyful news will come,
" Child, your Father calls—Come home!"

In the way a thousand snares
Lie, to take us unawares;
Satan, with malicious art,
Watches each unguarded part:
But, from Satan's malice free,
Saints shall soon victorious be;
Soon the joyful news will come,
" Child, your Father calls—Come home!"

But, of all the foes we meet,
None so oft mislead our feet,
None betray us into sin,
Like the foes that dwell within.
Yet let nothing spoil your peace,
Christ will also conquer these;
Then the joyful news will come,
" Child, your Father calls—Come home!"

THE WAY, HOPE, AND END, OF THE CHRISTIAN.

THUS far on our way to Zion
   We thro' grace divine are come;
And the Friend whom we rely on
   Soon will bid us welcome home.

Grace and truth our steps attending,
   Safe we still shall walk along,
Till, our destin'd journey ending,
   Truth and grace shall be our song.

Then these eyes, which now with sadness
   Oft in transcient clouds appear,
Shall be deck'd with beams of gladness,
   Never more to shed a tear.

Then these hearts, which now so often
   Not the sharpest threats can move,
Nor the sweetest words can soften,
   Shall be all dissolv'd in love.

Tho' we're still with foes surrounded,
   Foes that often damp our joy,
Christ, who has so often wounded,
   Soon will ev'ry foe destroy.

He who doth will yet deliver,
   Till we reach the happy shore,
Till we pass the gloomy river,
   Till we sigh and weep no more.

Then the mind, whose chief employment
  Is to watch and conflict now,
Favour'd with complete enjoyment,
  Shall with endless rapture glow!

Solid hopes like these possessing,
  Let us march with courage on,
Bold thro' fears and dangers pressing,
  Till we wear the conqu'ror's crown:

Till we wave our palms in glory
  Thro' the blissful plains above;
Till we sound the wond'rous story
  Of the GREAT REDEEMER'S LOVE!

AFTER PRAYER.

HOW sweet to wait upon the Lord
While he fulfils his gracious word;
To seek his face, and not in vain;
To be belov'd and love again!

To see, while prostrate at his feet,
Jehovah on the mercy seat;
And Jesus, at the Lord's right hand,
With his divine atonement stand!

" Father," he cries, " I will that these,
Before thee on their bended knees,
For whom my life I once laid down,
Be with me soon on this my throne!"

Amen, our hearts with rapture cry,
May we with rev'rence look so high!
Ascended Saviour, fix our eyes
By faith upon this glorious prize!

With this delightful prospect fir'd,
We'll run, nor in thy ways be tir'd;
And all the trials here we see
Will make us long to reign with thee.

And as we pass along we'll sing
The grace of our ascended King;
Thy sceptre with delight obey,
While with thy sword we fight our way.

And when thy sweet, thy awful voice,
In death invites us to rejoice,
Thyself, O Saviour, strike the blow
That slays our last, our strongest foe!

Thou didst thyself perfume the grave,
From fear of death thy saints to save;
Thyself thro' Jordan's billows guide
Our souls, and stem the rolling tide!

Thyself conduct us to the land
Where trees of life in order stand;
Where bliss, a sea without a shore,
Forbids the blest to wish for more!

THE TRIUMPH OF FAITH.

YE faints, that bow at Jefu's feet,
   In heart and tongue the fame,
Hofannahs fing, in concord fweet,
   To our atoning Lamb!

Aloft, beyond th' etherial dome
   That clips this pond'rous ball,
Let praife afcend, till Jefus come,
   And heav'n's bright curtains fall.

Yet, when each orb in yon blue fkies
   Shall fet to rife no more,
More loud and fweet our fongs fhall rife
   To him we now adore.

When the bright heav'ns, in liquid fire,
   Shall melt and burn to drofs,
O'er all their ruins fhall afpire
   The ftandard of the crofs.

There fhall the radiant armies flock
   Whom Jefus calls his own,
Nor tremble at the mighty fhock
   That hurls creation down.

Firm as the everlafting hills
   Remains the finner's friend;
The faith which now our bofom fills
   Shall there in glory end.

When angels shout—" To judgment come!"
 And God's just wrath proclaim,
The bloody sign shall wave us home
 To our Jerusalem.

CHRISTIAN TRAVELLERS.

PILGRIMS we are, to Canaan bound,
 Our journey lies along this road;
This wilderness we travel round
 To reach the city of our God.

And here as travellers we meet,
Before we reach the fields above,
To sit around our Master's feet,
And tell the wonders of his love.

Oft have we seen the tempests rise;
The world and Satan, hell and sin,
Like mountains seem'd to reach the skies
With scarce a gleam of hope between.

But still, as oft as troubles come,
Our Jesus sends some cheering ray,
And that strong arm shall guard us home
Which thus protects us by the way.

A few more days, or months, or years,
In this dark desert to complain,
A few more sighs, a few more tears,
And we shall bid adieu to pain!

FAITH

FAITH FEEDING ON REDEEMING LOVE.

SAVIOUR of sinners, from thy death
Our spirits draw their heav'nly breath;
Thy dying groans with life abound,
And healing flows from ev'ry wound!

Thy sorrows are a fruitful tree,
Whereon rich blessings grow for me:
Thy spotless life a golden mine,
Where all my brightest treasures shine.

Out of thy fulness we receive
The grace and faith by which we live;
Thy broken body is our food,
The wine we drink is thy rich blood.

Thy righteousness is all our dress,
In which, before thy Father's face,
Perfect in beauty we appear,
Without one spot to raise a fear.

No holiness of life or thought
We know, but what thy grace has wrought;
And thy good Spirit makes us do
Our heav'nly Father's will below.

Not unto us be glory, Lord,
But to thy Spirit and thy word;
Salvation is alone of grace,
And grace alone shall have the praise!

ADMIRATION AND CONFIDENCE.

AND may I hope that, when no more
These pulses beat with life below,
I shall the God of life adore,
And all the bliss of being know!

I who deserve no place but hell,
No portion but devouring fire,
Shall I with Christ in glory dwell,
Possest of all I now desire?

Will God, who never could endure
On sin to look without a frown,
With a kind smile pronounce me pure,
And grant me an immortal crown?—

Will Jesus own a wretch like me,
And tell to saints and angels round
That, when he suffer'd on the tree,
My sins augmented ev'ry wound?—

Will he from life's eternal book
To earth and heav'n proclaim my name;
On me as on his children look,
And make my lot with theirs the same?—

Will Jesus, as my surety, place
Before his Father's glorious throne
Me as an heir of sov'reign grace,
Me as his own adopted son?—

He will!—I read it in his word,
And in my heart the witnefs feel:
I fhall be with and like my Lord,
'Tho' fin oppofe in league with hell!

I fhall be with him when he comes
Triumphant down the parting fkies;
And, when his voice breaks up the tombs,
Among his children I fhall rife :—

Among his children I fhall ftand
When quick and dead his throne furround,
Bleft with a place at his right hand,
And with immortal glory crown'd!

When all his foes beneath his feet
In chains of endlefs torment lie,
Unworthy I fhall fill a feat
Among the princes of the fky!

ADORATION OF THE REDEEMER.

JESUS, thy faints affemble here
Thy pow'r and goodnefs to declare;
Oh may thefe happy feafons prove
That we have known redeeming love!

And, while of mercies paft we fpeak,
And fing of endlefs joys to come,
Let thy full glories on us break,
And every thought give Jefus room!

E 5   Engrave

Engrave thy name on ev'ry heart;
And give us all, before we part,
The life-restoring joys to know
Which from thy veins in rivers flow.

No other food may we desire,
No other theme our bosoms fire,
But sov'reign, rich, redeeming love,
While here and when we dwell above!

Thine everlasting love we sing,
The source whence all our pleasures spring;
How deep it sinks, how high it flows,—
No saint can tell, no angel knows!

Its length and breadth no eye can trace,
No thought explore the bounds of grace;
Like its dear Author's name, it shines
In infinite unfolded lines!

The love which saves our souls from hell
On this side heav'n we ne'er shall tell;
But, when we reach bright Canaan's plains,
We'll sound it in immortal strains!

PRAISE TO THE KING OF ZION.

KING Jesus, reign for evermore
Unrivall'd in the courts above;
While we with all thy saints adore
The wonders of redeeming love.

No other Lord but thee we'll know,
No other pow'r but thine confefs;
We'll fpread thine honours while below,
And heav'n fhall hear us fhout thy grace.

We'll fing along the heav'nly road
That leads us to our blefs'd abode,
Till with the vaft unnumber'd throng
On Zion's hill we join our fong :—

Till with pure hearts and voices fweet
We caft our crowns at Jefu's feet,
And fing of everlafting love
In everlafting ftrains above.

THE PRIVILEGES OF A CITIZEN OF ZION.

ZION's the city where I dwell,
Surrounded by the hofts of hell;
But glory foon will be my home,
Where fin and hell can never come.

Till then among the faints below,
Where Jefus deigns his face to fhew,
Let me be favour'd with a place,
Conftant in all the means of grace.

No earthly city can compare
With Zion, when her LORD is there!
Her gifts like golden turrets rife;
Her fervent graces melt the fkies;

Her stately walls are girt with pow'r;
Safety and strength compose her tow'r;
Firm on a rock her palace stands,
The glory of the builder's hands.

A river, full of peace and love,
For ever flowing from above,
Makes her inhabitants rejoice,
And tunes with praise each mourner's voice.

Here all the graces live and reign—
A fruitful and a glorious train!
Their happy influence shed abroad,
And point us to their Author—God.

Faith, like an eagle from her nest,
Mounts up in search of heav'nly rest;
And love, like incense from a fire,
Ascends in flames of strong desire.

Patience, that long enduring, still
Submissive waits Jehovah's will;
And lively hope, that lifts her head
Beyond the regions of the dead.

Here all the heav'n-born sons of grace
Proclaim the King of Zion's praise,
Whose precious name from ev'ry tongue
Flows on in one delightful song.

Oh lovely place, where first my heart
Was taught for baneful sin to smart!

Where

Where first my eyes were brought to see
That Jesus liv'd and dy'd for me!

Here would I dwell, and learn to sing
The grace and love of Zion's King,
Till I ascend the heav'nly skies
And sing his praises as I rise—

Till in the palace where he reigns
I learn, in sweet immortal strains,
The wonders of that love to tell
That sav'd my soul from sin and hell!

The two following Pieces were occasioned by the Death of an only Son.

CHRIST's UNPARALLELED LOVE.

A FRIEND there is—your voices join,
   Ye saints, to praise his name!—
Whose truth and kindness are divine,
   Whose love's a constant flame.

When most we need his helping hand,
   This friend is always near;
With heav'n and earth at his command,
   He waits to answer prayer.

His love no end or measure knows,
   No change can turn its course;
Immutably the same it flows
   From one eternal source.

When frowns appear to veil his face,
　And clouds furround his throne,
He hides the purpofe of his grace,
　To make it better known.

And, if our deareft comforts fall
　Before his fov'reign will,
He never takes away our all,—
　Himfelf he gives us ftill!

Our forrows in the fcale he weighs,
　And meafures out our pains;
The wildeft ftorm his word obeys,
　His word its rage reftrains.

No hand can move in earth or hell
　Againft the foul he loves,
But as directed by his will,
　But as his love approves.

Then let him raife his chaft'ning hand,
　We bend beneath his rod,
Refign his gifts at his command,
　And ftill adore our God!

Silent be all my anxious fears,
　My heart no more repine,
Since Jefus in his bofom wears
　The flow'r that once was mine!

I'll love my Lord, and trust his word,
   Tho' he thinks fit to frown;
And bless the hand that holds the sword
   Which cuts my comforts down.

THE SAME.

WHEN Jesus both of God and men
   Was treated as a thief,
His body felt amazing pain,
   His soul amazing grief.

He bore our sins; our sorrows fell
   Like mountains on his soul;
Like rising seas he saw them swell,
   Like raging billows roll.

No weeping friend his bosom lent
   To rest his drooping head;
With gaping wounds his flesh was rent,
   His wounds unpity'd bled.

Alone he stood, alone he fell,
   Alone the Conqu'ror rose,
Alone he burst the bars of hell,
   And trampled on his foes!

He knows the heights of heav'nly bliss,
   The depths of earthly woe;
Acquainted well our Jesus is
   With all the griefs we know.

Himself

Himself to friends and foes a friend,
   No friendly hand he found,
That would the least assistance lend
   When dogs beset him round.

In heav'n they "Holy, holy!" cry,
   When Jesu's praise they sing;
On earth they shouted—"Crucify!"
   And mock'd the lowly King.

Alike unmov'd, he bends to wear
   Heav'n's praises as his crown;
Unmov'd alike, he stands to bear
   On earth his creatures' frown!

Meek as a lamb beneath the knife
   Of butchering hands, he lay;
And patiently resign'd the life
   They could not take away.

But, oh! it shook his soul with dread,
   And fill'd his heart with fear,
When God his Father turn'd his head
   Against his fervent prayer!

Why, O ye saints, ye sinners, why
   Did Jesus suffer thus?
In heav'n they shout—on earth they cry—
   "Jesus was slain for us!"

Our sins were laid upon his head;
    From us the burden fell:
Beneath our sorrows Jesus bled,
    And we are freed from hell!

His Father's all-pervading eye,
    That tries the reins and heart,
Could in his soul no blemish see,
    Yet did he make him smart.

For, tho' within his holy breast
    No blemish could be found,
With names that had the law transgress'd
    His heart was graven round.

There Justice read our legal debt,
    And summ'd the vast amount;
And Jesus plac'd, without regret,
    All to his own account!

The thunders of a broken law,
    While gath'ring o'er his head,
Unshaken our Redeemer saw,
    Tho' fill'd with holy dread.

Justice, that held the flaming sword,
    And found his bosom bare,
No drop of mercy could afford,
    Because our guilt was there!

THE GARDEN OF GRACE.

A Garden fenc'd from common earth
 By special sov'reign grace,
Enrich'd with plants of heav'nly birth,
 The Church of Jesus is.

His Gospel is the open sky,
 His love the shining sun;
Rivers of peace, which never dry,
 Thro' all this garden run.

His Spirit is the heav'nly wind
 That o'er this garden blows,
And, op'ning each immortal mind,
 The Saviour's image shows.

Faith, like an ivy, to the rock
 That stands for ever cleaves,
And thro' the tempest's loudest shock
 Eternal calm perceives.

Assurance, like a cedar, rears
 Its stately branches high,
Beyond the reach of doubts and fears,
 And blossoms in the sky.

Here love appears a fruitful vine,
 From Christ the bleeding root
Receiving life and sap divine,
 And bears immortal fruit.

Humility,

Humility, a lily fair,
  Tranſplanted from on high,
Grows here, perfuming all the air
  With ſweets that never die.

Firm patience, like an aloe ſtrong,
  By ſtorms unſhaken grows,
And, changing ſcenes enduring long,
  At length in glory blows.

Here hope, a lively evergreen,
  Diſplays her ſmiling face;
And flow'rs of ev'ry hue are ſeen,—
  But all are plants of grace!

HELP AGAINST THE FEAR OF DEATH.

WHEREFORE ſhould dark events alarm,
Or ſharp temptations make us faint?
The ſtrength of an almighty arm
Keeps and defends the weakeſt ſaint.

Yet, till this ſcene of action's clos'd,
And we lay down the ſhield and ſword,
We muſt oppoſe and be oppos'd
By thoſe who crucify'd our Lord.

But glorious will our triumph be
When the ſevere engagement's done,
And we, from ſin and ſorrow free,
Aſcending, ſhout the conqueſt won!

                        But,

But, oh! when swelling Jordan rolls,
Should Christ his lovely presence hide,
Will it not overwhelm our souls
Before we reach the Canaan side?

Who knows how deep the flood may be
When we our awful summons hear;
Or what dark prospects we may see
When his black banners Death shall rear?

Well, should the tyrant Death display
His ugliest form when we pass o'er,
Our skilful Guide knows all the way
From Jordan's brink to Canaan's shore.

Yes, the Redeemer once was dead!
And, when he pass'd the gloomy grave,
Death's blackest waves roll'd o'er his head,
That we might know his pow'r to save.

THE HARMONY OF CREATION AND REDEMPTION.

THE heav'ns above our heads declare
Thy glory, Lord, in letters fair;
With marks of thine almighty pow'r
Adorning each revolving hour.

The sun, when he begins his race,
The borders of thy works displays;
And, as his glories brighter shine,
More plainly shows thy skill divine.

Thy

Thy creatures' hearts with rapture bound,
While he with splendid speed goes round;
And daily, as thy bounteous hand
Sheds blessings down on ev'ry land.

The moon, that from her azure throne
By night diffuses light alone,
Thy separating skill proclaims
Wher'er she sends her borrow'd beams.

The distant stars, that thro' the night
From far emit their twinkling light,
Expand our views of thy domain,
And tell how vast, how wide thy reign.

The various trees, and plants, and flow'rs,
Born of thy heav'n-descending show'rs,
With fishes, birds, and beasts, unite
Thy name thro' earth and seas to write.

Creation's works, in all their forms,
From rolling stars to creeping worms,
In never-ceasing concord join
To sing thy name, thy pow'r divine.

But, when the dawn of heav'n we view
In fallen sinners born anew,
When in the gospel's brighter skies
We see the sun of glory rise,

No more we aſk the ſtars to tell
What Jeſus only could reveal;
In him at once our eyes behold
More than creation ever told.

Omnipotence, in accents ſage,
Creation ſings thro' every age;
But Love and Juſtice, Truth and Grace,
Shine brighteſt in Redemption's rays.

Thy nature and thy name we read
When on the croſs we ſee him bleed;
And, when we hear his dying groan,
His ſhame and ſorrow tell our own!

The luſtre of thy holy law,
Thus honour'd, fills our minds with awe;
And Calv'ry's ſcenes at once reveal
More love and wrath than heav'n and hell.

How pure the truth that would not ſpare
Thine equal, thine eternal heir!
How great the love that freely gave
Thy ſon thine enemies to ſave!

Thy juſt commands, by him obey'd,
In all their beauties ſtand diſplay'd;
Thy righteous vengeance falling there
Fills earth and heav'n with holy fear,

CHRIS-

CHRISTIANS HAVE REASON TO SING.

ARISE, ye saints, and sing below
In prospect of the joys above;
Think, while you mourn where sorrows grow,
On yonder world of light and love!

Jesus, the God that once came down,
And liv'd a man of sorrows here,
Now wears in heav'n th' imperial crown,
And waits to bid us welcome there.

And, ere we reach the happy shore,
His Spirit condescends to bring
A taste, to make us long for more,
Of that which makes the angels sing.

And, if the earnest of his love
We find while yet on earth so sweet,
What must the full possession prove
When round his glorious throne we meet!

When with immortal eyes we gaze
On the full glories of our God,
As in Emmanuel's face they blaze,
And fill with light the blest abode!

Why should the saints be fill'd with dread,
Or yield their joys to slavish fear?
Heav'n can't be full, which holds the Head,
Till ev'ry member's present there!

In heav'n the Head—the members here—
Ten thousand thousand, yet but one!
So far asunder, yet so near!
Some yet unborn—some round the throne!

How bright eternal wisdom shines
When it displays eternal love,
Instructing by those dazzling lines
The earth beneath and heav'n above!

A CHRISTIAN WELCOME.

WELCOME, dear brethren, to this place!
Be banish'd ev'ry slavish fear!
Ye come to seek Emmanuel's face,—
And he has promis'd to be here.

Seek him in pray'r—he'll surely come
To do us good before we part;
Each humble breast he'll make his home,
And dwell in ev'ry waiting heart.

He'll come with all his gracious train
Of lively graces bright and strong;
Then shall the Lamb for sinners slain
Sound loud and sweet from ev'ry tongue.

Oh then be earnest, take no nay,
He'll answer ev'ry good desire;
Give him your hearts—tho' cold as clay,
They'll melt like wax before the fire!

ON THE BIRTH OF EMMANUEL.

WHEN heathen pow'r its higheft pitch had gain'd,
And idol gods, of man's invention, reign'd;
What time Auguftus fill'd a peaceful throne,
And Satan call'd a captive world his own—
The Lord of lords, and heav'n's eternal King,
The Prince of Peace, whofe name archangels fing,
The greateft Hero earth has ever known,
Came down to claim the kingdoms for his own.
No armed bands before the warrior rode,
No clafhing fpears embru'd his path with blood;
Superior arms the heav'nly Monarch chofe
To crufh the pow'r of his rebellious foes.
The dreadful fword by which his foes are flain,
With ev'ry wound gives everlafting pain.
No founding trumpet call'd the world to war,
His peaceful herald was a filent ftar;
No fhouting rabble hail'd him from the fkies,
The fhining herald pointed to the wife;
The wife, obedient, left their native place
To feek the royal babe of David's race;
Then gladly at their infant Sov'reign's feet
Their gifts prefenting, with fubmiffion meet,
Worfhipp'd their King, tho' in a manger born,
While his own fubjects treated him with fcorn.
Yet, tho' neglected by ungrateful earth,
Celeftial armies fung Emmanuel's birth;

Angels obedient to Jehovah's law,
Who serve with love, and worship him with awe,
Proclaim'd to men the advent of their King,
And made the heav'ns with hallelujahs ring:
The echoing heav'ns to earth convey'd the sound,
And rous'd the watchful shepherds from the ground:
" Glory to God," the enraptur'd cherubs cry,
" Who dwells in uncreated Majesty;
" Peace and good-will to men, who dwell below,
" Henceforth in everlasting rivers flow."

CHRISTIANS, LOOK HOMEWARD.

DRAW near, O ye blessed, and help me to sing
    The treasures for you laid in store,
When at last you shall meet your dear Shepherd and
        King,
    To weep in this desert no more.

Oh think with what rapt'rous shouts we shall rise
    To join with the glorified choirs,
When Jesu's bright chariot appears in the skies,
    And death at his coming expires!

When " Come, O ye blessed," sounds sweet in our ears,
    By Love everlasting exprest,
What place will be found for our doubts and our fears
    In sight of the mansion of rest?

No more shall the wicked our comforts annoy,
  Nor conscience from guilt feel a wound;
No tree of temptation, our peace to destroy,
  Shall in the blest region be found.

No passions, unholy, our bosoms shall move
  To taint the fair mansions with strife:
Our Shepherd shall feed us on pastures of love,
  And lead us to fountains of life.

Look up, ye dejected, that weep as ye go,
  And complain that no comfort ye prove;
Cast down your sad willows, and sing while below
  Of the bliss that awaits you above.

Anticipate heav'n, it will sweeten those hours
  When sorrows all round you appear;
Will strew all the road to mount Sion with flowers,
  And smooth the rough path-way of care.

A DAY OF CHRISTIAN HOPE.

O MAY my future days be spent like this,
In expectation of eternal bliss,
In pray'r and meditation on the word,
Blest with the presence of my gracious Lord.
Borne on the wings of faith half-way to heav'n,
With grateful song for what's already giv'n;
Anticipating that which is to come,
And pressing forward to my heavenly home!

And doſt thou, O my ſoul, experience this?
Then heaven is thine, and everlaſting bliſs;
Heaven is thy home, and Jeſus thy delight,
Thy ſong by day, thy comfort in the night.
Sin is thy foe, yet death ſhall prove thy friend;
Thy joys ſpring there, and there thy ſorrows end:
Then ſhalt thou ſee, while cherubs round thee ſing,
In all his beauty, Zion's glorious King!
There ſhalt thou bid adieu to all thy cares,
For God himſelf ſhall wipe away thy tears.
Delightful habitation! bleſt abode!
Whoſe light is Jeſus, and whoſe temple God!
When ſhall I, with immortal eyes, behold
Thy living fountains and thy ſtreets of gold?
When on the banks of thy clear river tread,
While fruits of life hang ripening o'er my head?
When ſhall I ſee thy pearly gates extend,
And in my Saviour meet my God and friend?
When ſhall I anchor on thy bliſsful ſhore,
And riſe in day to ſet in night no more?

A DAY OF CHRISTIAN CONFLICT.

GO, trifling world, and leave me to my reſt,
Leave me, to be with Jeſu's preſence bleſt;
Give place awhile, ye tranſient earthly toys,
To higher pleaſures and ſuperior joys.
Go Unbelief, and hide thy horrid face,
Nor more oppoſe the work of ſov'reign grace:

Go,

Go, dark Mistrust, with all the gloomy train
That tinge my sweetest hours with bitter pain:
Hence, hateful thoughts, that poison all my peace,
Damp my best pleasures, and my fears increase:
Rebels against my sov'reign Lord, begone!
And leave me to enjoy my God alone.
Down to thy native hell, ungrateful sin!
While I the praises of my Lord begin.
Alas! in vain I bid the world begone;
In vain I strive to think of heav'n alone;
The very thoughts I wish to cast aside,
Ebb thro' my mind like a returning tide;
Till to the cross I turn, and there behold
The dying Shepherd of the heav'nly fold
Pour out the treasure from his bursting veins,
To purge my guilt, and wash away my stains!
See Justice pierce the bosom of my God,
And bruise his soul with an avenging rod!
" 'Tis finish'd!" with his dying breath he cries,
'Twas finish'd when he clos'd his languid eyes!
'Tis finish'd—all redemption's work is past,
Death lost his sting when Jesus groan'd his last;
Mercy and Justice kiss'd when Jesus dy'd,
And love sang triumph in the crimson tide.

AN ANSWER
TO ONE INQUIRING—WHAT IS HARMLESS?

HARMLESS if ever you would be,
To Christ the harmless you must flee;
And if from God your sins you hide,
It must be in his bleeding side.

Before your piercing eye can trace
The glory of redeeming grace,
The less'ning world must disappear,
And all your soul must centre there.

Ere heavenly pleasures be enjoy'd,
Delights of sense must be deny'd;
And faith must lend her eagle wings,
Till you look down on mortal things.

There is indeed no other way,
Whatever sensualists may say;
If, therefore, my advice you take,
For *this* all other ways forsake.

Tho' the deluding creatures smile,
Charm, and amuse your thoughts awhile,
'Twill leave a dreadful sting behind
To poison and torment the mind.

Where'er you wander up and down
Pale disappointment still will frown:
God has ordain'd no other rest
But this—Believe, and you are blest.

ELEGIAC

ELEGIAC THOUGHTS

On the Death of Mr. Samuel Dawson, *and Miss* Elizabeth, *his Sister, two pious and amiable young Persons, who died within ten Months of each other in the Bloom of Life.*

WHY should I the tear of sorrow
   To the new-dry'd eye impart?
Why disturb the barbed arrow
   Rankling in the parent's heart?

But when I behold the dwelling
   Where Eliza once abode,
Painful thoughts my bosom swelling,
   Thro' my eyelids force a flood.

Bitter is the sad reflection,
   Samuel was nipt in bloom!
But it crucifies affection
   To survey Eliza's tomb.

Samuel, as a tree in blossom,
   (Smiling summer just begun)
Open'd his expecting bosom
   To the church's glorious sun.

What an harvest had succeeded,
   Promis'd by so fair a spring,
Sunn'd and water'd, all it needed,
   Is not for the muse to sing.

But the pleasing expectation
   Early sown, and springing fast
In the breast of each relation,
   Perish'd by one fatal blast!

Little seen, but always growing,
   By a secret stream supply'd,
From the fountain ever flowing,
   Fair Eliza liv'd and dy'd.

While she liv'd, she liv'd a blessing
   To her mother's feeling heart;
When she dy'd, she dy'd expressing
   All a daughter's filial part.

From the father, from the mother,
   From the weeping lover's breast,
From the sister, from the brother,
   From the friends that lov'd them best—

Samuel and Eliza sever'd,
   Mounted to their seats above,
Where, with Christ's own presence favour'd,
   They unite to sing his love.

Jesus, who was slain to save them,
   Lov'd them better far than they,
And before his throne would have them,
   Tho' each bleeding heart said, " Nay!"

To those realms of peace and glory,
   Where their happy spirits rest,
Let each saint, who reads their story,
   Forward press till with them blest.

A SINNER's CONVERSION.

OH, the amazing depths of grace!
   Should I restrain my tongue,
The very stones would bid me blush,
   And burst into a song.

Engag'd with others, like myself,
   To spend an idle hour,
I went to see a sorcerer
   Exert his magic pow'r:

Then, while methinks stern Justice cry'd,
   Strike that young rebel dead—
Sheath thy bright sword, my Lord reply'd,
   I've suffer'd in his stead;

I've paid the debt thy law demands,
   My blood has quench'd its flame;
And (spreading forth his wounded hands)
   Bade Justice read my name!

Justice beheld, and sheath'd her sword,
   Which Mercy smil'd to see,
Took from his lips a gracious word,
   And brought it quick to me!

"Sinner,"

" Sinner," said Jesus, " thou art mine,
　" From everlasting, mine !
" I therefore henceforth will be thine,
　" To everlasting, thine !

" Thy enmity to my free grace,
　" Thy love to self and sin,
" Shall to my sov'reign love give place;
　" Here shall thy heav'n begin."

Twas him that by one potent word
　Call'd forth the cheering light;
'Twas him that bade the light give place
　To each revolving night.

My soul confest Almighty Love
　As chaos did before,
Felt the creating fiat move,
　And own'd the Saviour's pow'r.

So mighty was his princely voice
　When thus he spake to me,
That his command became my choice,
　Tho' I to choose was free.

Since then I glory in the cross
　Of my Redeemer slain,
And waste of time and perfect loss
　I count my former gain.

PRACTICAL AND EXPERIMENTAL

ESSAYS,

ON DIFFERENT SUBJECTS, IN PROSE.

ON DIVINE TRUTH.

THE glory of univerſal nature is truth; the ſubſtance of all truth is immateriality; and the evidence of the reality and glory of that which is immaterial is experimental truth. God is the ſelf-exiſtent ſpirit, the fountain of truth; and from him comes the word of divine revelation, the Bible, which it has been juſtly ſaid, is "The glory of our world;" as juſtly was it added, "The glory of the Bible is the goſpel;" and it may be farther ſaid, with equal propriety, The glory of the goſpel is, "Jeſus Chriſt, the ſame "yeſterday, to-day, and for ever;" who is emphatically, "*The* TRUTH," inaſmuch as in him centre all the rays of natural, hiſtorical, ſpiritual, and eternal truth. He is the only channel by which the glorious river of divine Truth flows down to this fallen world of ſinners from the unbounded ſea of God's everlaſting love. In the reflecting mirror of his mediation, ſufferings, and interceſſion, are clearly ſeen all the divine attributes glorifying each other in the ſalvation of ſinners, Pſalm lxxxv. 10. "Mercy and
"have

"Truth are met together, Righteousness and Peace have kissed each other." But though this be a general description of truth as it comes from heaven into our world, in particular cases it is always a relative term, and changes its appearance according to the subject to which it relates; as when it shews a sinner his danger, and a saint his safety.—In the first of these cases truth is as sharp as an arrow; in the second, it is healing as balm. "What is truth?" said Pilate to the great Redeemer; but, as though he feared an answer would confound him, he immediately hasted from the presence of the very object of his inquiry. What is truth? say many of our modern professors of divinity; but, when the mouth of divine revelation is opening to answer them, away they run to their own reason, which they worship, and blasphemously inquire whether divine revelation should be believed or not. But the word of God, which is "quick and powerful, sharper than any two-edged sword, dividing asunder the soul and spirit, and piercing even to the joints and marrow," will not leave pursuing these till it finds and proclaims them guilty of abusing its authority. There is a truth which, entering the human soul, causes such pain as many, who have felt it, have thought worse than the entrance of steel into the most tender and precious nerves of the body. The following is of this description;

The

The purity of the moral law, with its binding obligation upon men—The immutable juſtice of God—And the unavoidable certainty of his eternal vengeance againſt ſin, in the perſons of offenders. When a man that loves ſin, and lives in the practice of it, is convinced of the exiſtence of theſe truths, "A certain fearful looking-for of judgment and "fiery indignation" kindles in his ſoul an awful foretaſte of hell; and no wonder, for it is certain God can lay the burning cauſtic of conviction on a ſinner's conſcience, till reflection becomes ſo intolerable, that he chooſes rather to ruſh into hell by ſuicide, in hopes of finding in that diſmal cavern of eternal deſpair a refuge from the Omniſcient eye, than to abide on earth under its all-ſearching ſcrutiny any longer. Alas! how many who have felt all this will have no other branch of truth for the experimental ſubject of their everlaſting contemplation! Think of this while there is hope, ye who try to forget God, and attempt to hide yourſelves from the eye of revealed truth under ſome refuge of human invention. The final judgment of the world, and the execution of eternal vengeance, are both committed into the hands of the Redeemer; and ſhould he who ſends his ambaſſadors of mercy and peace to you in the Bible and the miniſtry of his goſpel be provoked by your ingratitude and unbelief to exerciſe the one and inflict the other, how heavy, from

ſuch

such a hand, must that just vengeance fall! Psalm ii. 12, "Kiss the Son, lest he be angry, and ye perish from "the way, when his wrath is kindled but a little." To which, for encouragement, is added, "Blessed are "all they that put their trust in him." But as, on the one hand, nothing can be so unwelcome to a natural man as the knowledge of the truth of his own case, on the other hand, nothing is so big with consolation to a spiritual man. The truth of a believer's state shews him rivers of joy and peace, which lead him on to an unbounded sea of bliss, unutterable in its quality, and eternal in its duration! As no truth wounds like the truth of God, so no truth heals like it. He who bears the arrows of divine conviction in the quiver of truth, and shoots them impartially from the unerring bow of his justice, diffuses as freely the balm of immortal life from the eloquent lips of his mercy. Matt. xi. 28—30, "Come unto "me, all ye that labour and are heavy laden, and I "will give you rest. Take my yoke upon you, and "learn of me; for I am meek and lowly in heart: and "ye shall find rest unto your souls. For my yoke is "easy, and my burden is light." John vi. 37, "Him that cometh to me I will in no wise cast "out." Verse 51, "I am the living bread which "came down from heaven. If any man eat of this "bread, he shall live for ever: and the bread that I "will give is my flesh, which I will give for the life
"of

"of the world." "God so loved the world, that he gave his only begotten Son, that whosoever believeth in him should not perish, but have everlasting life," John iii. 16. Rom. viii. 32, "He that spared not his own Son, but delivered him up for us all, how shall he not with him also freely give us all things?" With expressions like these the word of God abounds: these are but as a few drops taken out of the gospel river; and what can language add to them? Uninspired diction, conscious of its own deficiency, retires before the superior energy, simplicity, and authority of divinely inspired truth. Go, sinner, with all the eagerness of desire to live, alarmed into exercise by a sight of the arrows of death; go to the throne of divine grace, and request the application of these and other exceeding great and precious promises to thy guilty soul, and thou wilt find in these leaves of the tree of life a balm sufficient to heal effectually and everlastingly the deepest wounds that ever the unwelcome truth of God has made in thy conscience. The jailor, whose case is recorded in the xvith of Acts, is a striking instance of this; so is the thief on the cross, who was new born even while he was dying! What extreme anguish of body did he suffer even at the time when he requested this balm of life for his soul! Why did he not ask him who had so often raised the dead, and healed the otherwise incurable, to add one to the

number

number of his miracles by saving him from the bodily torments he then felt? This was the requeſt of his fellow, and at firſt it appears to have been his own; but when **the Holy Spirit** let one ray of divine truth into his dark underſtanding, he ſaw the worth of his ſoul, and the **glory of the Redeemer,** in ſuch a light as threw all his bodily concern into ſhades, and re**queſted no** other balm of the great Phyſician, but the balm of life to heal his ſin-wounded conſcience, **and** Chriſt's preſence and favour as the future portion of his immortal ſoul.

But even believers in Chriſt, who have no reaſon to fear Jeſus as their final Judge, are ſubject, while in the body, to many wounds which only truth can heal: **they are** wounded in the conſcience by **known ſin** in general; in the will, by perverſeneſs to the revealed will of God, which ought **to be** the only rule of a Chriſtian's faith **and choice; in the** affections, by deſiring **or delighting in** any creature or thing **contrary to the moral law; and** in the underſtanding, by **error. All** theſe wounds the **truth of God,** and that **only, can heal.** Each of theſe wounds, while it continues in the ſoul undiſcovered to it by truth, muſt get worſe and worſe; but though **the truth of a** wounded caſe muſt bring with it the pain of conviction, it alſo brings tidings of effectual relief. Is the conſcience wounded; what ſays Divine Truth to ſuch a one? " Come and let us reaſon
" together;

"together; though your sins be as scarlet they shall
"be as wool; and though they be red like crimson,
"they shall be white as snow." Wherein does this
reasoning consist? The Spirit of truth shews the sinner his wretched and helpless condition, and a free pardon flowing to him by the channel of Christ's atoning blood; and, under such a manifestation, the vilest of transgressors must feel a heaven of peace flow into his conscience in one moment. Guilt can no more exist before the presence of Christ in the soul, than darkness can look the sun out of countenance at noon day. If this is the language of divine truth, why do Christians so often go on mourning on account of guilt, and are not healed? They indulge a perverse will; this was the case of Israel when Jeremiah so pathetically cried out, "Is there no balm in Gilead? Is "there no physician there?" Taking both for granted, he continues his exclamation thus: "Why then is "not the hurt of the daughter of my people healed?" To look only on the conduct of some Christians might frequently suggest an interrogation like the prophet's; but the word of truth proves that such Christians are living below their high birth and privileges. There is no want of balm in the Gilead of grace, nor want of willingness or power in the great Physician to apply it: but those who are wounded in the will are more willing to be healed than to be searched; so much are even Christians like the silly ostrich, who, when

he

he is purfued, hides his own eyes, that he may not be feen. We cannot hide the truth of our cafe, be it as bad as it may, from our beſt friend, yet we are unwilling to unbofom ourfelves to him, through fuch a fenfe of fhame as it is a fhame to harbour. How does fuch conduct elucidate the words of our Lord, " The children of this world are, in their genera-" tions, wifer than the children of light!" that is, wifer about temporal things than Chriftians are about fpiritual concerns. But why fhould a wounded patient be unwilling to go to a kind and fkilful phyfician? The old monfter Righteous Self is unwilling to be ftript of all its glory, that Chriſt alone may have the honour due to him; and God the Redeemer will not give his glory to another. Jefus is a loving phyfician, but he is a faithful one; he has a tender hand, but he has alfo a fearching probe: and when we have fuch a view of his character, that the language of our fouls is, " Search me, O God, and try me, and fee if " there be any wicked way in me, and lead me in the way everlafting," there can remain no obftacle to our going to Chriſt with a wounded will: and going to him, we muſt receive a cure; for it is written, " Thy " people fhall be willing in the day of thy power." The affections of a Chriftian are wounded either by defiring fomething the Lord fees not fit to give to us, or by inordinate grieving after fomething which he has taken away: in the laſt cafe the wound is fometimes

times so deep that it seems as if a part of the heart itself was torn away with the beloved object; but this is a proof that the object thus removed had been put out of its place. Other objects may have a place in our heart, but none but God must have the possession of it: " My son," says he, " give me thine " heart." If therefore we give our hearts to another than himself, it is both wise and kind in him to remove the idol; and this is only breaking the cistern to make us drink at the fountain. Divine truth has a balm to cure this wound: " He hath sent " me," says Christ, " to heal the broken hearted." But let us remember, that when the Lord wounds the heart by taking away one idol, it will not do for us to supply the place of it with another, or with any creature-good. The wounded heart must be taken to the great Physician to be healed, and he will prescribe nothing less as a remedy than giving up all creature dependence, and being satisfied with God as a portion.

The understanding of a Christian is also subject to be wounded, which is done by the entrance of error in some specious form, so clothed as to impose itself on the mind for truth: and this is in some respects more dangerous than any of the former; for in each of those cases we can hardly help feeling that we are wounded, but in this we must remain insensible of our hurt; because as light in the understanding

gives

gives us a right idea of things, error therein is like an uneven glafs held between the eye and the object looked at, by which every thing we behold is mifrepresented. In the relief of such a cafe divine truth appears in its own native excellence. As a clear fky never wears a more pleafing afpect than on a ferene evening after a cloudy and ftormy day, fo never does the word of God prove more divinely precious than when, with triumphant rays, it fhines into the underftanding, and, fcattering the clouds of error, difperfes all the ftorms with which they threatened the benighted foul. Happy is the man who, whenever he feels a doubt begin to cloud his comforts, or fufpects an error in his underftanding, flies immediately to the fountain of truth, the Bible, for eftablifhment and information! Wifdom is his friend, and prudence his counfellor; and with fuch company he is not likely to run far aftray without being reftored to the right path again.

It is faid by fome that there grows not an herb in the field but what might be of medicinal ufe were all its qualities known; whether this obfervation be true or not, it is certain there is not a promife, precept, threatening, or reproof in the word of God, but what has both an object and an end in view. But as the wounded foot of the traveller may often tread on the very herb which, if fkilfully applied, would heal it, and yet remain uncured; fo by going to the Word

for

for comfort or direction, without afking the Holy Spirit to apply it to our hearts according to its own meaning, we often tread with unhallowed feet on thofe very fentences which are moft fuitable to our own cafe, without perceiving either their relative fuitablenefs to us, or their own inherent beauty; yea, in fuch a frame we look over *the Pearl of great Price*, without perceiving its ineftimable worth, or defiring to poffefs it as our own: yet even carelessnefs and irreverence may be cured by divine truth, for it is written, " He knoweth how to give " his Holy Spirit to them that afk it:" and it is farther written, that it is the Spirit's work to take of the things of Chrift, who is the truth itfelf, and manifeft them to the fouls of his people. It is true, Jefus is a judge, but it is equally true that Jefus is a Saviour. It is true God hates all iniquity, but it is equally true that through the blood of Chrift, as an atoning facrifice for fin, he pardons all the iniquities of the foul which flies to that precious blood for refuge.

TRUTH.

TRUTH, like an arrow from Jehovah's bow,
Conviction on its barbed point conveys
Swift thro' the heart of each rebellious foe,
And cuts a paffage for Jehovah's praife!

No stubborn sinner can the shock withstand;
No hiding place from Justice can be found,
When truth, impell'd by that unerring hand,
Transfixes conscience with a mortal wound.

Man may with man contend, but man with God,
Alas, how weak to urge unequal fight!
When, by once lifting his Almighty rod,
He puts ten thousand foes to endless flight.

How sharp the torment!—Sinners ponder here—
How sharp the torment they endure in hell;
The falsehood which they love, deny'd them there;
ETERNAL TRUTH's the sharpest pang they feel!

But, hark! what sounds of triumph rend the skies!
The upper skies, where holy angels dwell!
How strong the contrast to those gloomy sighs
Which echo from the hollow caves of hell!

Ten thousand thousand high-born seraphs sing,
Ten thousand thousand blood-bought saints reply,
" Worthy to reign is Truth's immortal King;
" And let him reign to all eternity!"

How shakes the soul, appall'd with guilty fear,
Which hell's eternal groan with horror thrills!
How much too lofty for a mortal ear,
The notes which sound from yon celestial hills!

My

My foul, to which of thefe (for one muſt be),
To which of thefe fhall I henceforth belong?
Shall I for ever howl in mifery,
Or fwell the choir of their triumphant fong?

Examine well the bent of thy defire;
For as the feed is, fuch the tree will prove:
Sin grows to ripen brambles for the fire—
Grace fwells the bloſſom, and the fruit is love.

Yet, fin-fick fouls, no more indulge defpair,
Truth has a balm to heal the wound it gives;
Jefus, who dy'd, truth's glory to repair,
To make thofe glory's known, for ever lives!

This is the tree of life, whofe vital bloom
Thro' all the foul diffufes healing pow'r;
This, to the confcience, brings forgivenefs home,
And guilt's vindictive curfe is felt no more.

ON DIVINE ZEAL.

THE zeal which men feel when they are warmly engaged in fome earthly caufe or party, burns generally with a furious, violent, and blind determination to bring about the ends they propofe, be the confequence what it may: but the holy zeal which the Lord the Spirit kindles in a new-born foul, and which confifts in an honeft and intenfe concern for the

the glory of God, burns with a clear and steady flame; its eyes of knowledge being so wide open that it can even distinguish between offences and the persons offending. It is grieved whenever the Lord's name is dishonoured, especially when it is done by his own people's lukewarmness; in this it is like Christ himself. Rev. iii. 16, The sight of a lukewarm church makes it sick; but oh how it rejoices to see believers' lamps of profession well trimmed and burning clear, when at the same time their loins are strengthened by the girdle of truth. It is angry with nothing but sin; yet is never so well pleased as when the glory of God is promoted in the salvation of sinners. It is a living coal taken from the altar of heaven, and will burn up all that opposes its way back to that altar again. What is there that may not be done with heaven in our eye and earth under our feet? with Christ, the captain of salvation, to say, "Go forward," and his Holy Spirit to shew us the way in which we should walk? Divine zeal knows how to watch and to wait when it is necessary, but cannot bear to let opportunity of doing good pass by without embracing her; yet, if it sit long looking out at the window of inquiry without seeing this fair damsel at all, it is apt to pine and grieve after her; and no wonder, seeing they were born for each other, and never meet without joining hands, or part without earnestly desiring soon to meet again. This divine

zeal,

zeal, when called to it, will go through evil report with equal cheerfulness and serenity as when it goes to meet a good name: and, whenever it is so circumstanced that truth or itself must suffer, it will go through floods or through flames to save divine truth from the hands of violation.

ON CHRISTIAN WATCHFULNESS.

EVERY Christian is called to be a watchman, and is commanded to watch, having his loins girt about with truth, and his lamp burning with zeal for the Redeemer's glory, as one that waits in constant expectation of his coming. A Christian should watch with confidence, because Christ will certainly come again according to his promise—with constant expectation, because it may be soon—with patience, because it may be long—and with submission, because Christ, a sovereign, has a right to come whenever he will. This character, when applied to the Christian, is far from an unmeaning one; for he is never left without something valuable to watch over, and something dangerous to watch against; he has to watch over the work of God in his own soul, that it stand not still, as a chastisement for his neglect; and over every Christian with whom he has any influence, that none of them may turn aside from the good way without a friendly and timely warning from him: and he has to watch againſt three different hoſts of enemies—the world, out of which he is called by divine grace, and from which he is commanded to live ſeparate, but which is always attempting either to allure or alarm him back again—Satan (whoſe captive he formerly was, and out of whoſe power Chriſt delivered him), together with all the infernal powers of darkneſs—and laſtly, his own depraved nature, which is conſtantly hankering after the ſervice of his old maſter, and the corrupt enjoyments of a ſinful world, but which he is commanded, by the Captain of ſalvation himſelf, utterly to deny, mortify, and even crucify to death, without the leaſt degree of pity or partiality.

Having theſe precious things to watch over, and theſe dangerous enemies to watch againſt, how ſhocking, in ſuch a character, muſt the crimes of ſpiritual ſleep and ſlothfulneſs appear! A common watchman has only to watch the outer doors of the houſe that thieves break not in: but a Chriſtian has both the outer door of his ſenſes to watch, leſt thieves break in; and the inner chambers of his heart, leſt traitors break out. But there is a circumſtance peculiar to the Chriſtian watchman, and to him alone; he has nothing to fear from either, or even both, of the hoſts of his enemies without, ſo long as the traitors within are not ſuffered to make a league with them. Who then (being employed as a watchman in ſuch a caſe, a case, and having an exact account to render, not of what is done without, but of what is consented to within) would spend his time and attention in walking round a thousand outer doors, while the only dangerous one, the inner door of the heart, must remain both neglected and exposed? In vain do we watch over our actions, if the spring of those actions, the motive with which they are done, is all the while neglected. Pride may slip on the coat of charity, and pass for a servant of Christ before our eyes; Self may put on the robe of Christ's righteousness, and strut before us undetected, being mistaken for well-grounded assurance; the fear of man may sneak into the corner of cowardice, from the heat of the battle, having on the specious garb of lowly humility; Covetousness may walk abroad in credit under the cloak of Frugality; and even Lukewarmness may pass for cautious Prudence, till Christ, the searcher of hearts, is sick at the horrid sight, before the soul itself is even sensible of its danger! In vain do we watch over our words, important as the duty is, while we neglect their fountain, our thoughts; for how can he that knows not what he thinks understand what he says? Yet, needless as this question may appear to some, how little is the duty of self-government in this respect understood? Every good thought which enters the mind is a friend, and brings some good thing with it; and every bad thought is a thief, and comes to take some good thing away. Were these things generally believed, how gladly would Christians welcome the one of these guests, and how cautiously would they watch against the other. Others judge of a man by his words and actions; and they can, in this state of things, have no better rule: but he that would form a just judgment of himself must turn his eyes inward, and consider on what it is that he constantly delights to think, and what subject it is that to dwell on, in his meditations, affords him most satisfaction. No man but him who thinks with order can be ready to speak at all times with propriety; yet the Christian is exhorted to be ready at all times to give an answer to him that asketh a reason of the hope that is in him, provided he do it with meekness and fear; and the scriptures of truth cannot exhort a man to do that which is not a duty: thinking with order is therefore a Christian duty, and of course a Christian privilege. It may be asked, Is not this an hard thing to attain to? It may be difficult of attainment at first, but when once it is wrought into habit in the soul, it becomes, like all other duties, not only easy but delightful. It is written, "The way of "transgressors is hard;" and this observation is equally just when applied to confused and incoherent thinkers; for as the wicked find more trouble in committing sin than the just in the path of obedience,

so

so the man that will not take pains to think with order, has more trouble from inconsistent and unconnected thought, than he that watches over the first motions of his mind has in bringing his thoughts into order. Laziness in thinking is inconsistent with solid peace of mind; for true peace consists in a consciousness of friendship with God through a Mediator; and the constant assurance of this requires and includes the utmost activity of soul, inasmuch as it certainly requires a right understanding of our own case and state, of the complex person of Christ, and of all the attributes of God as glorified in our salvation. But to go farther still; the heart of man is the fountain from which thoughts, words, and actions, spring; and the Christian watchman is exhorted to keep his heart with all diligence, as out of it are the issues of life. " As a man thinketh in his heart " so is he," says the word of God; and Christ himself said, " Out of the abundance of the heart the " mouth speaketh." " Out of the heart proceed " evil thoughts, murders, adultery," &c. &c.——— Thoughts are but the images of desired objects formed in the mind, but the desire of the heart itself is the former of those images. It is the heart that is said to be " Deceitful above all things and desperately wicked," so that it is added, " Who can " know it?" This then is the inner-door at which the Christian watchman should stand, and inquire of every thought as it rises, whence it comes, and whither it goes. All the desires of the heart are either of the reptile or winged kind, and are known to the diligent soul by their inclination, which is either to creep along the earth after some carnal object, or mount up towards heaven, where Christ is. Earthly desires are like moles, they cannot see their own way, or what will be the end of it; but heavenly ones are like eagles, they can look at the sun in his full strength, and see clearly to the end of their own aim, the attainment of heavenly-mindedness, and the enjoyment of God in Christ as a portion.

ON COMMUNION WITH GOD.

COMMUNION with God is the highest possible enjoyment of a creature in heaven or on earth: but there are different degrees of it; sometimes it is experienced to such a degree, even here, that all earthly care and all creature affection and regard are for a while swallowed up by it; it includes at once a display of the perfections of God to the soul, and the soul's interest in those perfections. Jehovah is so infinitely capable of making his intelligent creatures happy, that he can in one moment, though he find the soul in the deepest gloom, fill it with joy unspeakable and full of glory. Communion with God is the essence of Christian experience. Flavel said, he
learned

learned more in one hour's intimate communion with God than in many years experience beside. Union to God by faith in Christ is essential to communion with him. It is the glory of God in the face of Jesus which Christians behold while they abide on the mount of communion with him. It may not be improper here to inquire, what are peculiar marks of close communion with God? The mind is deeply tinged with the following colours of heavenly die; reverence, satisfaction, and devotion: Reverence is the very highest pitch of humility in its strongest exercise; it is the veil of the virgin soul in which it appears before Christ: satisfaction is the domestic habit of heaven, and devotion is the employment of that place. Though these are perfectly exercised only in heaven, they strongly mark the soul when it is near the Lord. These are connected with and rise out of each other. We cannot reverence what we do not approve; and in this case approbation must rise into satisfaction, because it is approbation of a portion; and, if I have a just sense of the dignity of God's character, and am satisfied with his fulness, I shall naturally and necessarily be devoted to his service, on whom I depend for all things, and from whom I receive all these peculiar blessings. To a soul that is near to God, the whole concern of time appears like the lessening shores to one on board a ship under full sail; they diminish till they are quite out of sight.

Suppose the sun should rise at midnight, and in one moment display the full glories of noon, this sudden transition from darkness to light would be but a feeble metaphor to convey a just idea of the Redeemer's glories breaking through the clouds of guilt into the believing soul! As a strong wind passing through a barn-floor bears away the chaff with it, so when that heavenly wind the Holy Spirit comes into the mind of a Christian, all the concerns of time fly before his presence, and the whole soul becomes an habitation for God.

A REMARK OR TWO ON THE SCRIPTURE DOCTRINE OF ELECTION.

WITH men election is generally understood of many electing one; with God it is *one* electing many: with man it is a transient act, and for a limited season; with God it is eternal. The root of election is God's everlasting love. Election itself is God's sovereign choice of some men to certain salvation. Heaven being the palace of God, is of necessity so pure and holy that none but pure and holy beings can be admitted there; and surely God has a right to choose his own domestics, seeing he must both purify and clothe them before they are fit for his presence. Man is so averse, since the fall, to holiness

and

and purity, that none but God can make him fit for heaven. God is under no obligation or necessity of nature to do this for any, since all are born, and live, and die (unless grace prevent it), in perfect enmity to him. Though it be an act of God's mind, not ours, a knowledge of it is essential to the enjoyment of that fine serenity or order of soul which is justly called the full assurance of faith and the earnest of our inheritance. What can shake the soul whose hopes are riveted to the promise of immutable Omnipotence? Who can erase the name of an elect soul from the eternal record of heaven? How may a redeemed soul, standing on this rock of eternal ages, exult in the certainty of its future triumph over sin and hell! and not only so, but in the certain prospect of the everlasting and uninterrupted enjoyment of the friendship of God!

Why is election so much spoken against?

Partly owing to the ignorance, and partly to the enmity, of men against the government of God. If a just king was hated by his subjects in general on account of his love of justice, those whom he would choose by calling them to enjoy, execute, or proclaim his rectitude, would be hated alike with him on the same account. The Jews attempted to plunge Christ down a steep precipice for only hinting at this doctrine, by relating a circumstance or two of particular and distinguishing Providence. Men do not like

like to think of God, neither do they like that God should think of them; and as they do not like abstract thought of God's infinite purity and justice, so neither do they like the miniature of those perfections in the lives and conversation of good men. Their enmity to this work of grace in itself stirs them up to speak against its fountain, election. Pride, self-righteousness, and envy, have much to say against election; Malice, founded not on the impropriety of the thing, but on their dislike of it. Pride, which loves to be high, says it lays man too low. Self-righteousness, which loves to be something, says it makes nothing of man, in that it makes not him to choose God, but God him. Envy, which neither aims at true happiness, nor can bear to see others happy, calls it a partial doctrine. And, seeing that with all these characters the whole world abounds, what wonder is it that election is every where spoken against?

ON THE EVIDENCE OF DIVINE GRACE.

AN evidence of divine grace is nothing less than the almighty voice of the eternal Spirit of God in the soul of man. "Let there be light," said Jehovah, "and there was light," even in the place where darkness and confusion dwelt before. Let there be life in that dead soul, says the divine Redeemer, and immediately

immediately his Holy Spirit irradiates and quickens the dark and lifeless powers of the mind, and he becomes a Christian. Should any one ask, whether there may not be an evidence of grace short of this; the scriptures answer—No: "Except a man be born again "he cannot see the kingdom of God." Not that every Christian has an equal degree of evidence of his celestial birth: there may be life where there is but little health and strength; but this does not render health and strength less desirable or useful: but as the same voice may speak aloud at one time and only whisper at another; whether it be a voice so loud as to produce full assurance, or so soft a whisper as only to produce the faintest holy emotion in the soul, such as love to the brethren, or even an inward struggle against sin, still it is the voice of the same Spirit. If a seed had no life in it, it could no more put forth a single leaf, or the smallest bud, than bear the choicest fruit; though it will be allowed it requires more sun and rain to produce the *latter* than the *former*. All the shrubs in the garden of grace are ever-greens, and all the fruits everlasting, because alike produced by the eternal Spirit, in consequence of an everlasting covenant ordered in all things, and sure. The weakest of God's children possesses (could he but perceive it) as real evidence of grace, and consequently is as safe as the strongest. Let us here consider what are meant by the graces of the Holy Spirit, as actually existing in the heart of a real Christian. The graces of the Spirit are the divine furniture of the soul, which is called the temple of the Holy Ghost; in other words, holy dispositions wrought into habit in the renewed heart by the same Spirit. They are so many little mirrors, each one reflecting some feature of the Redeemer. Paul calls them the fruits of the Spirit, " Love, joy, " peace, long-suffering, gentleness, goodness, faith, " meekness, temperance," and adds, " against such " there is no law," Gal. v. 22, &c. As many lights together hinder not each other's shining, but equally unite to produce a general illumination, in exact proportion to their number and size; so these graces obstruct not each other's growth, but spring in harmony each one from its own root, and each one bearing fruit peculiar to its own nature. All these spring from the one pure principle of love to God and man, which is planted in the soul by the regenerating power of the same Spirit, who carries on the work of sanctification till it is complete, and glorification crowns the whole. This divine principle of love in the soul shews itself by the going out of holy desire after spiritual objects, both in a way of affection and imitation. Holy desire in the soul shoots forth into holy action, and as holy principles lead to the choice of holy company and conversation, so holy company and conversation put us in mind of heaven, and

make

make us long to be there; and in proportion as these holy longings of soul proceed from an experimental knowledge of the fulness of Christ and the true nature of the glories of heaven, they prove the Christian is heavenly minded and growing in grace.

A FEW THOUGHTS ON SOCIAL RELIGION,

Humbly proposed to the Consideration of all Christian Congregations, particularly those denominated Baptists *and* Independents.

THE strength and beauty of social religion are founded on, and consist in, similarity of character, union of interest, unity of heart, and harmony of conduct: but similarity of character cannot be known without frequent comparison of sentiment; union of interest cannot be well understood without frequent comparison of evidence; unity of heart cannot subsist but by means of mutual knowledge and reciprocal communication; neither can there be harmony of conduct in many, but as far as in all their actions they keep one end in view, or act from one pure motive. Our divine Lord represents simplicity of motive, or a single eye, as the substance of human wisdom: "If thine eye be single, thy whole body "shall be full of light." What a shade of dishonour

does

does this saying cast over all human policy; which is but too much imitated in the conducting of religious societies, even churches where the gospel is professed in distinction from all ceremonies of men's devising! Perhaps the best of men fail more in this point than in any other. It is hard for human wisdom to consent to be melted down and cast into the mould of gospel simplicity. Respectability of character among men is one of the most refined baits the devil uses to catch Christ's fish with. But it is a truth, which must be felt sooner or later by every true Christian, that every degree of conformity to the world tends to make him a coward before men, and a slave before God. Gospel simplicity and true humility form the best basis for free communication in spiritual things. He that can look down on the simplest means of Christian fellowship, walks too much on the lofty mountains of self-esteem to gather many of the lilies of pure humility which grow in the valleys of social love. Social religion is the nurse of all the graces of the Holy Spirit in the souls of believers; and those who have been most under her care can witness with me that she is not a dry nurse. Is it not pity that in this one point the fellowship of saints on earth one with another should so far resemble that of the church militant with the church triumphant? We have infallible testimony that the saints in heaven are members of Christ's mystical body,

body, and as such we love them; but we cannot convey our ideas of divine things to them, nor receive from them any account of the felicity, or manner of their blissful state, that is reserved for us, till we **are as they.** So we have credible testimony that the members of the several churches to which we belong are Christians, and, as far as we believe it, we rejoice with them in the common salvation; **but we** have few means among us, as churches, whereby we **can** convey our ideas **of** divine things freely to each other, so as to enjoy literal fellowship. **Yet** as there can be no **wound in Zion but there is balm in** Gilead suited to heal it, let those, who **are convinced of** the truth **of** these observations, apply to the great Physician **of** souls, requesting him, who alone has sufficient skill and power, to send health and cure **in** this respect **to** his churches.

The instruction and establishment **of the** members of Christ's mystical body in the knowledge and experience of all that pertains to his spiritual kingdom, especially in the knowledge of Christ himself, his near and vital relation to them, **and** all the benefits and blessings which flow to them through the channel of his mediation—the oneness of their interest, as different members of one head—their unity of heart, frequent fellowship one with another as the mean of keeping alive and increasing that unity—their observance of the Redeemer's positive institutions, and

obedience

obedience to all the moral precepts in his word, I conceive to be the great ends which should be constantly kept in view, in the use of all the means of grace; and these ends can never be answered by an outward form of keeping together the church of Christ, though that may be both needful and useful in its place: yet the most that can reasonably be expected from the exercise of such a form of church discipline, or government, as it is sometimes called, is an outward appearance of peace, and a decent attention to each other in a way of common or intimate civility: such means may keep up the peace which stands opposed to outward confusion; but they are not likely to promote that peace which is built on mutual knowledge and good understanding, and which stands opposed to envy and discontent. Frequent heart-fellowship, and much delight in each other, are the beauties of church order: "By this," said our Lord, "shall all men know that ye are my "disciples, if ye have love one to another."

The fellowship of the church, as recorded in the Acts of the Apostles, appears to have been maintained by the love of Christ shed abroad in their hearts, and made known by much delight in each other's company, and free communication both of things temporal and spiritual one with another. And Paul, in all his epistles to the churches, keeps these things in view in a way of positive precept,

while

while outward difcipline may, in general, rather be faid to be implied than expreffed by him.

It has been, and will perhaps ftill be, objected by many, when fuch doctrine as this is advanced, that the Lord's people in general have not time or opportunity for frequent focial interviews, and that fuch things are apt to break in upon the order of families: but thefe objections, if clofely examined, will be found to be excufes, rather than reafons. What calling is there which ought to take the lead of our heavenly calling? What is the advantage of laying up earthly treafures, compared with that of increafing in the wifdom which cometh from above? And what the order of private families to the order of the great family of heaven, the church of Chrift? "The Lord loveth the gates of Zion more than all "the dwellings of Jacob." The order of families is without doubt of great importance; but the filence of fcripture refpecting the time and manner of it, is a fufficient reafon why it fhould always be attended to in fubordination to the more important Chriftian duties of public worfhip and focial fellowfhip.

I take the liberty of ftating here a few reafons for frequent and intimate focial worfhip. Chriftians were all involved in one fad ftate of depravity and condemnation; and they are all called by divine grace to look to one object for life and eternal falvation; that one object of their hope being fo highly exalted

that

that every one may look to him by faith at once without the leaft occafion of jealoufy, or interruption from each other, any more than there is for an individual to conclude that the light of the fun is not his becaufe every one is at liberty to enjoy the fame bleffing. The Redeemer paid one price for the ranfom of all his people; and the fame Almighty Spirit makes Jefus, as a complete Saviour, manifeft to them all; and as they are all faved and fanctified in one way, fo they are all going to one everlafting home.

The man Jefus loved his church even to his own death, and has left it this commandment, " Love
" one another, as I have loved you." " He that
" hath my commandments and keepeth them, he
" it is that loveth me; and he that loveth me fhall be
" loved of my Father; and I will love him, and will
" manifeft myfelf to him." And again, " As the
" Father hath loved me, fo have I loved you; con-
" tinue ye in my love." And again, " This is my
" commandment, that ye love one another, as I have
" loved you. Greater love hath no man than this,
" that a man lay down his life for his friends :" it appears that from this word the apoftle drew his reafon for faying, " We ought to lay down our
" lives for the brethren." The fame apoftle, I think, fomewhere fays, " Love is the fulfilling of the law." From thefe, and many other fcriptures, it is plain that love is the fubftance of all practical and ex-
perimental

perimental religion; and, from the nature of divine love in the heart of a Chriſtian, it is evident that ſocial religion is its heaven upon earth. Not only man, but all creatures, are made for ſociety, and without the preſence and mutual enjoyment of each other would be comparatively miſerable: but the delight which ſprings from Chriſtian fellowſhip is peculiarly exquiſite, as well as peculiarly laſting; its foundation, its author, its nature, its motive, and its end, all conſpire to render it incomparable and inexpreſſible! If theſe things are true, why have not the members of churches, in the preſent day, more knowledge of, and fellowſhip with, one another? Oh that ſuch a query were ſtarted by the Holy Spirit himſelf in the heart of every individual of that deſcription! Suppoſe ſuch a plain and honeſt inquiry were even to become univerſal among Chriſtians, would not the anſwer be ſomething like this? Tradition has ſet his foot on the heel of revealed truth, and has by this means ſo trodden off the ſhoes of the preparation of the goſpel of peace from the feet of the ſaints, that they cannot walk in the paths of ſocial love ſo well as they were wont to do. If any one aſk us why we worſhip in public during ſuch and ſuch hours on the Lord's day? it is enough that we can anſwer—Cuſtom and our own convenience have inclined us to the obſervance of thoſe hours. But ſhould any one ſeriouſly inquire of us why we have few, if any, means

of

of intimate and actual fellowship one with another as children of the same family? what a pity is it that we are equally obliged to answer in this case as in that—Custom and our own convenience have inclined us to the neglect of these. Was this the manner of the primitive Christians? No. " They con-
" tinued daily from house to house in fellowship, and
" breaking bread, and in prayers." Religion was their one concern; and, in attending to that one concern, though in number they were so many thousands, they were but one.

As for the usefulness of those meetings of the Lord's people, commonly called experience and conference meetings, I believe it is known, wherever they are judiciously and zealously attended to; and this is perhaps as much as can be said of even preaching itself. In the former of these meetings the Lord's people are found saying to their brethren, as David of old, " Come all ye that fear God, and I
" will declare what he hath done for my soul." And many are the advantages attending this lovely conduct: the various devices of Satan to entangle and perplex the minds of believers are exposed; the influence of earthly things on the mind is confessed, and mutually lamented before the Lord; the frequent deliverances the saints experience in times of trouble are recorded to the manifest honour of their great Deliverer; the faithfulness of a covenant God in an-
swering

swering prayer, and honouring them that honour him, is abundantly testified; the power of the cross of Christ to crucify sin in the heart is declared; the usefulness and suitableness of the preached word is acknowledged; love is increased; faith is strengthened; hope is enlarged; and a foretaste of heaven itself is often experienced on earth: even when the people come together with their hearts comparatively cold, reciprocal and free communication is often like the striking together of a cold flint and cold steel, and there comes out fire; as, saith the wise man, "Iron "sharpeneth iron, so doth the countenance of a man "his friend."

In the latter of these, called conference meetings, the light the Lord is pleased to cast on his own word, while his people are reading it from day to day, is set forth for mutual edification with much advantage; while he that exhorteth, according to the apostle's advice, waits on exhortation.

The holy scriptures are a mine of spiritual truth without a bottom; and as the divine Spirit is the only infallible expositor of them, and opens them to whom he will, the neglect of conference meetings seems to have in it the nature of quenching the Spirit in the hearts of the saints. On this subject I beg leave to recommend to the serious consideration of those who have in any measure the conducting of church affairs in their hands, the xiith chapter to the

Romans,

Romans, from the 3d to the end of the 8th verse, the whole xiith chapter of 1st Corinthians, and the ivth chapter to the Ephesians. I humbly conceive that no impartial Christian, whom God has favoured with the gift of discerning truth for the benefit of others, can deliberately examine those and many other portions of God's word, and yet believe the neglect of conference meetings, especially in large churches, to be an innocent thing.

So great is the loss which the churches sustain by the neglect of these things, and so great would naturally be the mutual advantage of reviving their use, that whoever may be the honoured instrument of so good a work, he may be justly called, in the language of prophecy, "The repairer of the breach; the re-"storer of paths to dwell in."

SENTENCES AND OBSERVATIONS

ON CHRISTIAN EXPERIENCE AND PRACTICE.

REMEMBER always to prefer the darkest shades of *truth* to the brightest beams of *fiction*.

WHAT a difference is there between a Christian in his own spirit, and a Christian in his own place!

THOUGH the law of God is a broken rule, it is not therefore a bad one.

PSALM cxix. is a honey-comb of sweets, all drawn from the inherent beauties of the moral law.

I HAVE been more than seven years learning to hold the bridle of judgment over the neck of affection, and am but a dunce at it yet; but this I have learned, that affection is strong, and judgment useful, when united, though each is comparatively nothing alone.

THE Lord's gifted children are like bees, they are constantly employed in sucking honey from the flowers of wisdom, and storing it up in hives for the use of the whole church.

NO Christian can possibly pursue his own true interest while he neglects or opposes the general good of the church of Christ.

THE Lord sometimes takes away his people's worldly riches, which thieves might have stolen, and gives it back to them in promises drawn on the fulness of Christ, which thieves cannot steal.

IT is better to be the Lord's servant than the church's idol—It is better to be the Lord's servant than the world's master.

I SHALL

I SHALL be rich when I am emptied of myself, and filled with my Redeemer's glories.

THE flowers of wisdom are constantly springing out of the ground of truth before the eyes of the enlightened understanding, from whence they are gathered by the hand of Faith, and placed in the bosom of Love.

THERE is a spring at the bottom of every doctrine of scripture, which, when we dig down to it, flows so plentifully into the mind as to furnish it with a continual succession of new and edifying ideas, and all these springs are supplied from the inexhaustible fulness of the *Mediator*. Who then need go a warfare at his own charges? or who can be in want of fresh matter that lives near this fountain? Who would be afraid of drawing all the water out of a well that has no bottom to it?

MINISTERS are barren, and Christians unfruitful, when they forget that Christ is the vine, and they are the branches—when they look for substance in themselves, and find only shadow.

THE strongest graces in a Christian soul are only shadows of the excellences of Christ.

HE

HE who is strong in the grace which is in Christ Jesus, need not be afraid of engaging in any good work; but he who thirsts to excel in the wisdom of the world will be a constant slave to the lust of praise.

HOW can we walk without Christ, who is our way?

HOW can we be sincere without Christ, who is the truth?

HOW can we live without Christ, who is our life?

HOW can we grow up into Christ's image, without being engrafted into Christ the living vine?

HOW can we increase, without receiving out of his fulness, in whom all fulness dwells, even all the fulness of the Godhead bodily?

IF "Be strong in the grace which is in Christ "Jesus" means, Be strong in confident expectation of receiving every necessary supply for future work and worship out of his fulness—who, but an unbeliever, can continue weak?

AS the influence of the rain and the dew on the vegetable world is not confined to the time it is wet by it, so the benefit of our good frames is not lost with their sweetness, but continues as long as we live, and, in a large sense, for ever.

WHEN the soul sees much of Christ, and has no opportunity of communication, it is ready to say, I am like a flower that blows in secret, and " wastes " its sweetness on the desart air." But the Lord says to such a soul, Am I not most glorified when my flowers bloom where I plant them? And is not my notice and approbation singly and alone more than that of all my creatures? Under such a kind reproof the will bends to the sovereign will of Jehovah, and the soul blushes confession and approbation at once.

THE sceptre with which Christ rules the world and governs the church is composed of all the jewels in the moral law.

THE smell of the flowers of paradise makes the way to heaven pleasant; and the sweetest flower in paradise is the Rose of Sharon, whose very name is as ointment poured forth.

IN the battles fought by men some must win, some lose; but in the Christian conflict every fighter wins.

HOLINESS is likeness to God, Christ is the image of God, and believers are the image of Christ.

IN the great and glorious work of making redemption manifest to men, Christ Jesus, the King of Zion, himself rides in the chariot of salvation with the bow of Omnipotence in his hand, the quiver of truth filled with arrows of conviction at his side, the fountain of everlasting love in his heart, and his eyes fixed on his Father's eternal decree to save his own people, while his Almighty Spirit, like a celestial dove hovering over his head, waits to wing every arrow he shoots into some chosen sinner's heart. What then is left for the ministers of the gospel to do? Their work and their glory is to run before his chariot crying to sinners, "Bow the knee;" and with his saints to unite in shouting, " Hosannah to the Son of " David."

IT is dangerous to run very fast after any thing but God, who has promised to hold up the soul that seeks him.

THE nearer a foul gets to God, the more it fees of its own fpots.

ONE that often handles gold will not highly efteem brafs; nor will he that drinks frequently the richeft wines be likely to covet water. How then can the profeffor who covets much of this world's good pretend to be rich in faith?

A CHRISTIAN is fulleft of God when moft emptied of himfelf—ftrongeft when he efteems himfelf weakeft—richeft when he is moft fenfible of his own poverty—faireft when he fees moft of his own fpots—and ftands leaft in need of reproof when he is moft difpofed to bear it.

THAT man is of all men the leaft likely to obtain true happinefs who makes prefent gratification his chief concern.

WHY fhould a Chriftian wifh to be in heaven before his time, when fo much of heaven is to be had on earth in the ufe of the means of grace?

THE fineft flower will lofe a great part of its beauty if you drop it among the dirt; fo will the fweeteft frame of mind a believer ever knows, if it fall into the ditch of pride: the heavenly flower,
Communion

Communion with God, will keep longest and smell sweetest while watered at the fountain of humility.

THE nature and perfections of God in Christ have the same effects on the Christian as the magnet on the steel; they draw his soul upwards.

GOD and his works are alike in this, the more narrowly they are inspected the more beautiful and glorious they appear: Man and his works are alike in this, the more closely they are inspected the more their deformity is exposed.

THE more a man seeks to find out God with his carnal eyes, the farther he gets from him—the more he seeks him with spiritual eyes, the nearer he gets to him.

THERE is but one way of fleeing from the wrath to come, and that is by the cross of Christ— but one door into heaven, that is his mediation—but one robe in which we can appear acceptable before God, that is his complete righteousness—and but one hand skilful and powerful enough to guide us by this way, in at that door, and adorn us with this robe; that is, the Holy Spirit.

LET the proof of God's love in your heart be his glory in your life.

ENVY looks at other men's comforts through a microscope, which exceedingly exaggerates them; and at his own through the diminishing end of a telescope, which both lessens and sets them at a distance—He looks at the bright side of other men's lot, and at the dark side of his own.

PRUDENCE, lend me thy cloak to hide the little zeal I feel for the honour of Christ from the eye of the multitude, till Providence opens the door of opportunity, and gives it occasion to come forth with advantage.

THE promises of God's word are like a garden of ripe fruits and sweet flowers, and the precepts are fine level walks, by which you may come at the one to pluck and eat, and the other to smell and admire.

EVERY sinner that knocks for admittance at the door of Mercy in the name of Jesus, is sure to find access to God and acceptance with him—Whose fault is it then that some will stay away?

THERE is no motive to obedience so strong as the full, rich, free, and everlasting gospel. The law,

like

like a magistrate, whips men to duty, and they perform it like slaves; but the gospel constrains a man to give up his whole soul, body, and spirit, with all that he possesses, as a living sacrifice to God the Redeemer, which he performs cheerfully, and esteems it but a reasonable service.

SELF-KNOWLEDGE is at the foundation of all true knowledge.

SELF-GOVERNMENT is at the foundation of all true government of others.

NO man can truly possess any thing without him, but in proportion as he possesses himself; neither can any man enjoy any thing which he does possess but in proportion as he enjoys his own being and capacity.

HOW great then must be the enjoyments of a regenerate man compared with those of a natural man, seeing it is impossible to know our own place in the system of God, without a true knowledge of the God of the system?

HOW can Christians be wise, righteous, holy, or free from slavish fear, without living on his fulness who is of God made unto them wisdom, righteousness, sanctification,

tification, and redemption? This being the true character of Chrift, might he not well fay, "Without me ye can do nothing?"

IS it a difcouraging thought that Chriftians can do nothing without Chrift, feeing they can do all things by his affiftance?

WHAT need have Chriftians to wifh to create good things for themfelves, feeing they can have every good thing of God, the Creator of all things, by afking for it in their Surety's name?

WHY fhould a Chriftian be backward to give, who has nothing but what is freely given to him?

THE richeft and moft valuable gems require the niceft care left they be loft or ftolen, and the higheft polifhed metals the ofteneft rubbing: fo the comforts of the Holy Spirit in a believer's foul are choice jewels; but there are fo many thieves watching opportunity to fteal them, that he who is not watchful indeed feldom keeps them long: and fo alfo the graces of the Spirit, which bear the fineft polifh that ever adorns the human foul, unlefs they are often revived by him that formed them firft, are fure to be fo cankered and rufted by fin that their very exiftence is not eafily difcerned.

THE

THE heavenly-minded Christian's communion with God is not like the shining of a rocket, gone before it is distinctly seen, but like a lamp well supplied with oil, burning steady night and day.

IT was not Peter's sinking which made him doubt, but his doubting which made him sink.

DOUBTING is not grace, nor the evidence of it; but as vermin are frequently most numerous where good things are kept, doubts often swarm in the soul where there is grace: yet as vermin swarm most where there is most neglect, so doubts prevail most in the soul where there is least watchfulness.

HOW could Israel of old keep near to God without looking to the pillar of cloud by day and the pillar of fire by night? And how can the Christian keep near to him without looking to Jesus, the light of his people, in the day of prosperity and in the night of affliction, conflict, and temptation.

CARNAL comfort thrives most in darkness; but divine comfort flies into the believer's soul upon the wings of divine light.

IT is certain that sin and the human soul are so united that none but God can separate them; but it is

equally

equally certain that the union between Christ and his people is so strong that God will never separate them.

CHRIST came to make peace by the blood of his cross, not that he might take it away to heaven with him, but that he might leave it on earth with his disciples.

A CHRISTIAN finds the joys of salvation the sweeter for all the intervening sorrows he feels; how sweet then will heaven be to him after all the troubles of the wilderness!

WHEN do we most enjoy the good things of Providence? When our passions are most harmonized and regulated by the spirit of divine grace.

WHEN is the world kept in its own place by the Christian? When it is most out of sight.

WHEN is heaven kept in its own place by the Christian? When it is full in his view.

> I most enjoy this transient world
> When all its glories prove but shades,
> That picture to my longing soul
> The world whose glory never fades.

COMMUNION with God is to a Christian as the apple of his own eye, tender and precious; yet, though it is natural to the new man to desire and prize this great blessing, it is equally natural to the old man to desire more of this world than is likely to consist with his frequent enjoyment of it; and hence arises a conflict which will continue more or less till the old man of sin is dead.

INDWELLING Sin is like a lion with whom the new-born soul is appointed to dwell during this life; and when this lion can get plenty of prey to keep his full strength in exercise, he will frequently roar so loud that the trembling Christian fears he himself shall even be devoured by him: but when the Christian watches all his motions, and takes away his food, with intent, if possible, to starve him to death, he often prevails so far as to enjoy himself in peace, and entertain spiritual guests without being disturbed by a growl from him; yea he will even get on the outside of his den, and exult, unmolested, in prospect of the death of this old monster.

THE great things of this world are for the most part, to him that possesses them, like a book of the finest paper bound in a cover of gold, with disappointment written on every page.

WHEN you have occasion to reprove a Christian friend, do it with the naked sword of truth; but first dip it in the balm of love, that while it pierces it may also heal.

JUST reproof, well timed, is a greater proof of friendship than even just commendation a little out of season.

FAITH is stronger than Samson and bolder than David; for it has often overcome that which conquered Samson, and faced that, undaunted, which David was sometimes afraid to meet.

FAITH comes from heaven; and though the whole world, with all the powers of darkness, unite to block up the path, back to heaven again it will fight and force its way.

A MAN in a state of nature is, as it respects spiritual things, like one who has been all his life shut up in a close prison without light; and, when the light of divine truth finds its way through the walls of his dungeon, it is hard to say whether he is most struck with the misery of his own self-ignorant situation, or with the glory of the light by which he discovers it.

THE

THE same light which shews a man that he is nothing in himself, shews him that Christ is all in all.

NO man can properly look for any thing else till he has found himself; and no man can find himself without a light from heaven.

FAITH seems to be like an uniting medium between the use of natural means and the working of miracles. It does more than all nature united, without it, could do; yet it does nothing by its own inherent power, but is the use of means still.

THE object of a Christian's hope is so all-sufficient and so highly exalted, that the whole church may look to him and trust in him at once, without the least interruption or occasion of jealousy one of another.

WHAT would man be if he was what he should be? What he was first made, the image of God, the picture in miniature of his Maker's perfections.

A MERE professor of religion is like painted flowers and carved fruit; he has the shape and the colours, but neither the smell nor the sweetness of real life.

THE image of Christ in the soul of a believer may for a time be covered with a cloud of tranfient obfcurity, but it will never be wrapt in a fhroud of eternal darknefs.

A MAN fhould not examine the word of God to know what he thinks of it, but to know what it fays of him.

THE higheft authority on earth is divine revelation; and the higheft authority in heaven will never contradict it.

CHRISTIANS live fo to the Lord while you live, that what you collect and diftribute in your journey through life may compofe a fweet wreath of flowers to perfume your memory when dead, and you will be fure of a noble funeral.

IT is faid of the wicked, " God is not in all his " thoughts:" but it may of the clofe-walking Chriftian, God is uppermoft in all his thoughts; for when he attends to his own temporal concerns he thinks of God indirectly, as having chofen for him his lot, and fixed the bounds of his habitation; and when he attends to what he likes better, worfhip, he thinks directly of all the perfections of God as they fhine forth, and are mutually glorified in his own falvation by the mediation of Chrift, the Redeemer.

THE greatest courage before men, and the deepest reverence before God, are highly consistent and even congenial.

WHEN you behold a countenance constantly graced with serene smiles, and expressive of inward satisfaction, it is likely that countenance is the window of a house where Christ dwells.

THE Atheist, who denies the existence of a God, is equally dependent on God for his own existence and support, and equally amenable at his bar of justice with the man who prays to God and praises him every day.

THE Deist, who boasts in his own light and despises divine revelation, is indebted to the very revelation which he despises for the light of which he boasts; for all the natural knowledge in the whole world is but the moon-light of the Bible, which is the sun of truth.

THE Socinian, who denies the atonement of Christ, must either be saved from his sins and the punishment due to them by the atonement he denies, or perish without remedy.

THE Arian, who denies the divinity of Christ, and yet professes to take refuge in his atonement,

must

must either be saved by the God-man Emmanuel, or come under the weight of this divine threatening, "Cursed is the man that trusteth in man, and "maketh flesh his arm:" to speak plainly, he must either be saved by God in human nature, or be damned without hope and without help for ever.

THE Professor, who denies the glorious doctrine of election, will nevertheless be saved everlastingly as a chosen vessel unto Christ, or be cast away, and rejected as reprobate silver : though, as his safety does not depend on the form of his creed, but on the strength of his Saviour, his disbelief of election does not render him non-elect, while his entire trust in the God-man Jesus proves him a real Christian.

SAYS Satan to a Christian, Thou art not sound in the faith, thy hold of Christ is not sure, thou wilt be lost and go to hell at last. Says the Christian to Satan, If my salvation depended on my hold of Christ, thou mightest chop off my fingers, and I might drop into hell; but as it depends on Christ's hold on me, chop off his fingers if thou canst!

AS the oak strikes deeper root and takes firmer hold of the ground the more it is shaken by storms; so true faith, the more it is shaken by temptation the faster hold it takes of Christ.

ALL

ALL striving to do without Christ, in every degree of it, is sin in the sight of God, whether it be found in the person of believers or unbelievers.

THE church will never be very rich in the wisdom which cometh from above, while the wisdom of this world is too highly esteemed by her.

AS the light of day would be of no use to us if we had no eyes to see it with; so Christ, the light of eternal life, is of no use to a sinner till the Holy Spirit opens his eyes, and shews him his need of a Saviour.

CHRIST is the only light by which a man can see to read his Bible right.

TRUTH is like the finest gold; burn it as long as you will you cannot reduce its weight.

HE that carries with him, as ballast to keep him from lightness, the golden weights of divine truth's importance, needs no addition from the leaden weights of human discouragement.

CHRIST is the only light by which a man can see himself, and the only light by which he can see God: the only light by which a sinner can see to make

make his escape from hell; and the only light by which a saint can see his way to heaven.

THERE was more light exhibited on, and diffused from, the cross of Christ, than ever was contained in, and diffused from, the sun, moon, and stars, throughout the universe; and perhaps it was therefore that none of those luminaries were permitted to shine while Christ, the SUN OF RIGHTEOUSNESS, displayed in their own operations all the perfections of Jehovah.

UNREGENERATE men say, they cannot see what light there is in Christ, who calls himself the light of the world: no more can a blind man see the light which comes from the sun; but, as his blindness does not prove that there is no light in the sun, so neither does the natural man's ignorance of the glory of Jesus prove that he is not glorious.

A SOUL without Christ is like a stomach without food; he may hunger, but he cannot be satisfied: for, as he is immortal, nothing can fill his desires but " the bread of God which cometh down from " heaven, that a man may eat thereof, and live for " ever."

THE

THE light which is in Chrift is not only informing light, but transforming light; it not only shews a sinner what Chrift is, but it makes him like him: it not only makes a blind man see, but it makes a dead man live.

MAKE time serve you as wings to fly to eternity.

GOD can polish the soul of one Chriftian so that other Chriftians can see their faces in it, and by this means difcover to them, for their encouragement, their own graces, and for their humiliation, their own fpots.

REVERENCE without rapture, in religion, is better than rapture without reverence.

RAPTURE and rapture is the experience of a child in grace; rapture and reverence that of a father.

STREAMS of divine favour and drops of demerit, make a fine mixture in a Chriftian foul.

INFUSE but a few drops of the pure fpirit of eternity into a large quantity of the water of time, and it will make fo ftrong a potion that the water can fcarcely be tafted.

I WAS

I WAS a little while ago on the wings of delight in God; but the afflicting hand of Providence has brought me down, and made me feel my feet, and now I find it hard work to walk a rough road without fainting: yet, as it requires more strength to walk under a burden than to run without one, I am encouraged to believe the Lord is with me still.

THE Christian's motto is, Get good, do good, and give God the glory.

LOVE is the only bond of everlasting union; and were the law of love in full force among mankind, no other would be needful.

LOVE is the distinguishing characteristic of a true Christian, and without it no man can have or give evidence that he is one.

LOVE is the element of heaven, and the only element of true delight to an intelligent creature.

THE living water of which Christ spake to the woman of Samaria, not only quenches the thirst of the mind after earthly objects, but inexpressibly cheers and strengthens the whole soul; so that it may be said, with the strictest truth, No man knows the true enjoyment, worth, or employment of his rational

and

and immortal exiſtence till he has drank of the water of this river of life.

THE Goſpel is good news from heaven; it is God's "Come up hither," ſpoken to poor ſinners, while in his word he ſhews them Chriſt as the ladder by which to aſcend—It is a proclamation of free pardon to deſerters, from the camp of Jehovah, who have enliſted into the ſervice of Satan, but are willing to return to their colours—It is a boat put out to ſhipwrecked ſouls—It is a city of refuge for the guilty, to hide them from the avenger of blood—It is an aſylum for the miſerable and helpleſs, and an eternal home for loſt wanderers—It is glory to God in the higheſt, and on earth peace and good-will towards men.

THE fear of God is like the rod of Moſes which ſwallowed thoſe of the magicians—it ſwallows up all contrary fears, and makes the righteous as bold as a lion.

ON WISDOM.

THE wiſdom which comes from above appears, when taken in the largeſt ſenſe, to conſiſt in operative ideas of the excellence of God's government, and the glories of redeeming love. The government of God

God includes his making and publishing laws for his creatures—his choosing their lot—his honouring their obedience—and his righteous punishment of their transgressions. An operative idea of the beauty and excellence of an object produces love to it. If we have such an idea of God's government in the universe, we love the Governor, and that love will shew itself in the following things: Love to his precepts as the rule of our actions—Satisfaction with our lot in providence, as chosen by him who has infinite wisdom to know what is best for us, and infinite love to incline him to give it—Lively zeal for the glory of his name in our actions—Joy in the honour and benefits with which he crowns obedience—and an entire acquiescence with his righteous will in punishing disobedience in the persons of his rebellious creatures. All this, and more, if possible, is included in an operative idea of redeeming love. The soul that feels itself redeemed, loves to give itself back to the Redeemer in every action of life: the love of God the Father in electing, the grace of God the Son in redeeming, and the work of God the Spirit in regenerating and sanctifying sinners, is the subject of its daily contemplation and delight. The man of whose character this is a just description is a wise man in the estimation of God, though all men should account him a fool.

ON COMMON LIFE.

SO univerſal is the love of fame,
That infamy itſelf is oft preferr'd
To dark obſcurity.——Methinks I ſhine,
The vain heart whiſpers inward to itſelf,
And, could the world my talents but perceive,
The world muſt ſure admire—Then oh for means
To burſt the ſhades and be a public ſtar!
But Poverty forbids—that iron chain
Binds many a ſwelling heart within due bounds,
That fain would flutter on the breath of fame,
And baſk in the broad beams of public praiſe.
Thus poverty, deſpiſed as it is,
Sometimes does good, where riches would do harm.

THE END.

This Day is *Published, in Octavo, Price* 2s. 6d.

REDEMPTION,

A POEM, IN FIVE BOOKS.

By J. SWAIN.

LONDON:

PRINTED FOR THE AUTHOR;

And sold by J. Mathews, Strand; Murray, Prince's-Street, Soho; and by the Author, No. 20, Bunhill-Row, Moorfields.

www.ingramcontent.com/pod-product-compliance
Lightning Source LLC
Chambersburg PA
CBHW031446160426
43195CB00010BB/871